The Mechanics for Breakthrough Success

The Guide to a Life You Never Considered Reachable

Thomas O'Grady, Ph.D.

The Mechanics for Breakthrough Success. Copyright © 2016 by Thomas O'Grady, PhD

All rights reserved. Printed in the United States of America. No part of this book may be used or reproduced in any manner whatsoever without the written permission except in the case of brief quotations embodied in critical articles and reviews. For Information, address Ping Enterprises, Publication Division, PO Box 3402, Redmond, WA 98074-4655

First Edition

Library of Congress Cataloging-in-Publication Data has been applied for.

ISBN: 978-0692697566

To Beth, who has more fine qualities than she could understand.

ACKNOWLEDGMENTS

Nothing is possible without the support of many people.

A great thank you and appreciation to many friends who have given me incites over the years as well as encouragement, not only for this book but for so many things.

My gratitude to my editor, Ron Roel, who started out as a considerate editor and became a good friend. Without his input and efforts, you would have a lot more difficult time enjoying this book. Thank you for your support and allowing me to express myself.

Thank you to my assistant, Joanne, who helped with everything from research to freeing my time to concentrate on this book.

Cover design by Stojan Mihajlov

Table of Contents

Success:
It's All Personal 1

Introduction:
The Kid with No Confidence 3

Part I: Self-Assessment 21

1. Is that *All* I Want to Believe? 23
2. Oh My God, You're a Parent! 35
3. Passion Can Suck...the Life Out of You 43
4. Are You Able? 57
5. Know Your Weaknesses—and 'Go on a Diet' 69
6. Limits Are Often Self-imposed 83
7. Developing the 'Why' in Life 93
8. How to Make Failure Not an Option 105
9. Wisdom Versus Knowledge 121

Part II: Taking Action 129

10. Set Your Goals by Reaching for the Stars, into the Unknown 131
11. Step Out of Your 'Comfort Zone' 145
12. Change Your Perspective of Yourself 159
13. Learning the Skill of Self-Motivation 169
14. Understand and Reduce Procrastination 181

15. *Yoku Mimin Suru*: Copy Well, 'Master What the Master has Already Done!' 197

16. Peers, Friends and Family can be Harmful 209

17. Program your Mind through Visualization 223

18. Don't Allow 'Can't' Into Your Vocabulary 233

19. Turn Jealousy into a Learning Opportunity 245

20. Whatever Happened to Sacrifice? 255

Conclusion **267**

21. The Next Level: Shoot for the Moon; True Breakthrough 269

While finishing this book, I had many ideas and thoughts for additional chapters. To say they will be in a future edition, doesn't help you. So, just go to the Book Site and register to get your copy of additional work as it becomes available.
http://www.MechanicsForSuccess.com

~ Thank you, Thomas

Success: It's All Personal

Before we get started, let me be clear about what I mean by success.

Success is not something I can determine *for* you. You have to determine it for yourself. Some people may decide that getting a college degree is important in achieving their career and life goals; others may decide to skip college and become ski instructors. While a college graduate may make more income and live in a better home with other things that money can get, they have given up some of their early life to reach those goals. The ski instructor may have less money later in life, but will have experiences and memories that the college graduate might not be able to have—even when they have the free time to ski every day—because they probably will no longer have the body to endure it.

Each of these paths is a personal choice. And as an economist, I would say that "success" means maximizing an individual's own choices or preference. It does not necessarily relate to some income level, but rather to both short- and long-term personal satisfaction. Who is to say that one person's choice is right and another's is wrong, as long as they accept the long-term impact of their choices? Success is based on your own preferences, even if you do not understand entirely why you chose a particular path at that time.

Whatever your choices, this book will help you find the breakthroughs to achieve those goals.

Introduction:
The Kid with No Confidence

When I was young, I never thought I could become anyone of significance. Other children dreamed of becoming engineers, lawyers, or scientists; I used to lie face down on my bed, hoping to become *average.* There were policemen and firemen in my neighborhood, but I never thought I could become a policeman, and I wasn't sure I could qualify to become a fireman—I didn't even know what it took to become one. Simply put, I had the lowest expectations of myself.

Looking back, that perception of myself seems quite strange—and painful. But I'm sharing these personal stories because they offer a window into the events that transformed my life, from someone who possessed no hope for the future to someone who is amazed at the successes he accomplished. The keys to a successful life are based on what I have learned while struggling to achieve my goals, including both the methods that helped me in challenging situations and the insights I gained with the help from many others. Some of the stories I'm disclosing are things that I couldn't even talk about 15 years ago. I tell them today in the hope that they will benefit others.

While I was growing up, my eyes were very crooked. People reacted to this trait by assuming that I was uncoordinated and stupid. While in Little League, I usually had the second-highest batting average on the team, yet when sides were chosen up on the street, I would usually get picked either last or next to last—just before the overweight kid who couldn't run to first base.

In junior high and high school, I had teachers who made fun of me in front of other kids in the class, maybe because they felt it helped them gain popularity with other students. Every year when my parents met with the school's guidance counselor, my so-called mediocre future was reinforced. The counselor would read off my high scores on the national or state aptitude tests. I had no understanding of the significance of the test scores. To me they were just another bunch of tests. Then, pushing the scores aside, the counselor would say something to my parents about not always being able to rely on tests, and not everyone being meant for college. The counselor would ask, "Have you ever thought about sending him to a trade school?".

Normally very shy, I vehemently insisted that they give me a chance, which they did—reluctantly. What was going through my mind at the time was not whether I was capable of success or how I would succeed, but the shame I would feel when my friends saw me placed in what was referred to as the "dummies class," usually inhabited by troublemakers and students who didn't really try.

Eventually, a few incredible coincidences helped change my life.

After a brief stint in community college, I joined the Army Security Agency. At enlistment time, everyone was given a battery of tests. In the second week of basic training, those of us in the Army Security Agency went to a special building to choose their careers.

When my name was called, I was greeted by an officer who immediately said, "We all know what you want: languages."

"No," replied, "I'm terrible at languages."

Actually, he said, I was very good at languages.

I told him that I took five years of German and never did well. (Admittedly, I didn't get along with my teacher, which was probably my own fault.) It turns out that I had one of the highest test scores the military had seen: 58 out of a possible 59. The overall average was 12 in the Army and 18 in the Army Security Agency, where on average the level of education was two-and-a-half years of college.

The officer told me that sending recruits to language school cost the government a great deal of money, and that only those who wanted to go were sent there. (I've been told by Army instructors it costs more than $1 million a year per student today.) He then told me I would be called back in a couple of weeks to see if I had changed my mind about studying languages.

This is when the first miraculous thing happened to me. Christmas was in the middle of boot camp and the army sent everyone home. On the train two guys about my age sat next to me and ended up inviting me to a New Year's Eve party in New York City. I had only been to a New Year's Eve party one other time; such gatherings always seemed silly. This time, however, I decided I would meet up with these nice strangers.

At the party, after I mentioned how I turned down the language school, excitedly they told me they had a friend who went to the language school in the military in Monterey, Calif. called The Defense Language Institute. They talked about how beautiful it was on the Monterey Peninsula. Most important to me, they told me that at the school I'd be taught how to learn a language.

When I returned to basic training, I went back to the Army Security Agency career building and while standing on the doorstep, I requested that my school and training be changed to foreign languages. The captain who answered laughed at me and told the colonel, who asked, you *actually* thought you could change your mind in the military. But after I answered a series of questions and they heard my score, they invited me into the building and called the National Security Agency. They promptly gave me my choice of languages—Russian.

All this, because I met two guys on a train. The rest of my life shifted based on this one incident.

While at the Defense Language Institute I bought an inexpensive car, and on weekends, I usually drove up to Marin County north of San Francisco to do some sightseeing and camp out. One weekend a fellow student asked if I would give him a ride home, since his house was on my way. This led to a second incredible coincidence. He lived in nearby Palo Alto. When we arrived at his house, his father greeted us and asked if I wanted to stay for dinner. Of course, I said yes. (Think: *home-cooked meal.*)

During dinner, my classmate's father asked me about the language school, then about my major in college and my SAT scores and language score. When I told him, he said, "You know, it is very unusual for someone to be gifted in both languages and mathematics." That didn't really mean much to me at the time. He then asked me if I was doing anything the next day. I said no, so he invited me to meet the comptroller of IBM. He explained that the comptroller might give me some ideas for my future career.

The next morning, I met with the comptroller and two engineers who worked with him. After we got to know more about each another, the engineers took me for a tour around IBM. At the end of the day, we returned to the comptroller's office. He told me that no matter what I was doing, wherever I was, at any time—during the service, college, summer time, before or after graduation, part-time or full-time—I could give him a call. And I would have a job at IBM.

Even after this event, I still didn't believe in myself. When enough people over a long period treat you as if you can never succeed, their influence is difficult to overcome. Still, it did get me thinking that if I worked very hard, I could perhaps, just perhaps, get a good job. This was only a single event, but it kindled a dream...and a little bit of self-confidence, a glimmer of hope, if I truly worked hard enough.

At the end of language school, while I was sitting with another student at a small coffee shop, one of the professors joined us. After a few pleasantries, he said, "Decide whatever you want to do, and you can do it. Whether it's law school or medical school or anything else, it is far easier than what you just went through." At that time, the threat of being failed out and going into the infantry was extreme.

So I started to wonder what I could do. Two concepts carried me through the next phases of my education and slow confidence-building.

First, I wondered: If it is true that humans use only 10 percent of their brains, could I make better use of my own? Suppose, for example, the average brain is rated at a performance level of 100 (thinking in terms of IQ), and suppose my own brain was only rated at 90. I really had no idea what it might be. Could I work my mind 20 percent harder than others? In that case, while others might have a brain performance rating of 10 (10 percent of a 100 IQ), if my mind worked 20 percent more than everyone else, my extra work would effectively produce a 10.8 performance rating, significantly higher than the others at 10. Whether this was biologically feasible didn't matter; it was my motivation.

Second, I thought about what I had just completed. At the school, there were people who had nervous breakdowns and others who had committed suicide because of the fear of failure and possibly going into a war zone. I thought, "If the military could get me to do all I did for their purposes, why couldn't I take that same energy, drive, and perseverance and use it for myself?"

Actually, it took eight more years before it began to really sink in that I was much better than the perceptions cast on me as a youngster. I continued to think that if I only pushed harder than everyone else could I *be something*; I needed to find out what that was and to push as hard as I possibly could. So I pushed, and the successes began to build, through the lingering doubts:

- I was promoted several times and put in charge of Russian language analysis for two-thirds of the former Soviet Union. I broke Soviet codes

three times and wrote two manuals on Soviet procedures.
  - I was awarded the Meritorious Service Medal – the same medal given to General Wesley Clark, Senator John McCain and General Norman Schwarzkopf, Jr.
- I became fluent in Japanese. It became far better than my Russian—I used to think and dream in Japanese.
- As a Hofstra University undergraduate student, I served as chairman of University Budget Committee and faculty representative to the Board of Trustees. I was a nominee for the Rhodes and Rotary Club Scholarships and the Danforth Fellowship (I was awarded the Rotary and withdrew from the Rhodes to get married).
- At University of California, Berkeley I received a PhD in Mathematical and Statistical Economics.

While in my third year at Berkeley, Gerard Debreu, a Nobel Prize-winning economist, asked me to do a dissertation under him. I had been in his class the previous semester. Usually, students run around trying to find a professor who will work with them. I spent a little time telling him I wasn't really good enough; he told me I definitely was, whereas I told him I did so well only because he was such a good teacher. The next day when I woke, I realized finally, I just might be better than I always had thought. Yes, it took eight years to overcome history and environment!

In subsequent years I went onto many more successful experiences:
- At GM Research Labs:
    - I extended the research done by Nobel Laureate Dan McFadden's work at Berkeley, applying it to Customer Perception of Quality. As far as I know, this was used for at least another 20+ years.
    - I developed systems for measuring demographic effects on car purchases, using techniques now called "data warehousing."
- I was hired away from GM by Chase to head Automotive Research and Forecasting.
    - Despite proclamations by the Chase president that profitability was impossible, we became profitable in 16 months.

- o As Chase was closing down all of its industry groups, I built a company.
- My company, Integrated Automotive Resources, eventually became the high-end firm in consulting with offices in Pennsylvania, London and Tokyo.
  - o As an analyst, I appeared on TV and radio hundreds of times, including all major networks and was quoted in the print media over 80,000 times including several other countries.
  - o Eight years before Oldsmobile was closed down, in a speech at an International Automotive Conference, I forecast their change of strategy would lead to their extinction.
  - o While everyone was wondering how fast Chrysler would die off as its stock price hit 9 1/2, I said it was about to make extraordinary profits. It did and the stock went up to over 71. The cutbacks and balance of expenses were huge.
  - o I called GM's inevitable problems ten years early, as I said they were entering a "death spiral."

- I was offered the position to head Volkswagen of Japan. While I had great admiration for Volkswagen and gratified by such a high compliment, I could not accept going to Japan at that time.
- I was invited by Microsoft to teach their own people data warehousing. I held all of Microsoft's top certifications and worked as a trainer to some major corporations, government agencies and brokerage houses.
- Then, I was hired by Microsoft, based on the track record of my accomplishments with other large Fortune 100 companies.
    - At Microsoft, I changed the Microsoft Training from just an update to product features, to what both the customers and Microsoft needed-a focus on developers' careers, which embedded their work into Microsoft products.
    - In the Windows organization, they decided not to create a service pack 2 for Windows XP and they shifted all resources, i.e. everyone to the next version of Windows. I took in upon myself to research their customer surveys showing that about 95%

of customer dissatisfaction was from XP. That work was used to reverse the decision, direction and resources that were already reassigned. With service pack 2, XP became a product customers liked and still are unwilling to leave.
- There are several other items that I'm leaving out but you can see the flow of careers.

I often think back to the string of coincidences that opened the doors to my life and gave me the ability to seek my potential. I took a test; I ran into two people on a train who urged me to go to the Defense Language Institute in Monterey. I gave someone a ride home, and his father happened to be the general manager of the West Coast branch of IBM. His father took an interest in me and introduced me to the comptroller of IBM. I happened to be sitting at a table with a fellow student when a professor joined us and gave us some unforgettable advice.

There are many people with similar stories of difficult childhoods and even more severe handicaps than I had. Many have not yet experienced life-changing coincidences or met the right people to guide them through their challenges. And I want to help those who have not had such opportunities—passing along my own life experiences so that they can change their own perspectives dream about what might be. If I can do it, they can too.

Even 10 years ago, I could not talk much about my experiences to anyone. Little by little, however, I felt more comfortable exposing my life as I saw how pieces of my story had a positive influence on others, particularly the military personnel with whom I shared it, not only to test my logic, but to inspire them.

This ability to share and best tell my story developed over time. I realized how much my life shifted based on just a few incredible incidents. While serving in the military, I was pushed way beyond what I ever thought I was capable of accomplishing. It was such a good experience that I often thought over the years how I accomplished certain things—and then wondered how to keep going further. In some cases, I learned just by reflection. I also learned from my own experiences. In a sense, I was my own laboratory of testing and experimenting. Lastly, I learned much from the writing and mentorship of others. All the time, I had broken out of my past and used it to accelerate my own progress. In the different areas that I became accomplished, I drew from all of these experiences. Each success was a breakthrough from my previous position and self perception.

The question that I tussled in my mind was, "How can I pass this on to others?" Wherever I am, I always try to encourage younger people, especially military personnel. Many of them don't know what they will do after leaving the military, so I started experimenting, speaking with active duty personnel who I happened to meet at airports.

I continue to ask them if they ever could have imagined being able to push their body and mind to do the things they did while in Afghanistan, Iraq, or elsewhere. They always say no. Many of them came from areas or backgrounds where they were not pushed as hard as they were in the military. Many of them had limited understanding of how far they can go, if they push themselves. I believe that if I can help them apply their experiences in the military to their life after the service, some of them can make breakthroughs like I did. I leave them with this thought: There are going to be tough times and many obstacles, and when you encounter those challenges, think back to that thought you had when I asked you about something you could not imagine being able to do until you actually did it in the military. When you come across something in your future that seems impossible, use that memory like a trigger. You can say to yourself, I did that, this is nothing in comparison. Then, prepare yourself to blow through that obstacle.

By relating my own story, I've often been able to motivate others to succeed in their own lives. At first, it was difficult to even expose a little of my background story. Over time, seeing the positive effects on some military personnel, I became willing to expose more and more of my past. The more I revealed, the more people related. In part, that experience is the motivation in writing this book.

I see too many people who are bright, but don't believe they can succeed. I understand that if people don't desire something more for themselves, that is personal preference or choice. But I don't like to see people resigned to lackluster lives because of unfounded beliefs and low expectations about their own potential.

I hope this book can influence people to change their outlook to work for their dreams. I know it takes considerable time and many positive experiences to overcome strong negative beliefs as it did for me. But as you read through the next several chapters, you can decide how much you want to do and what to apply to yourself. When taking the train to success, you can decide when to get off—and you can always catch a later train. Just remember, though, that if you take a later train, it will, of course, arrive later. If you start earlier, the outcome, like compound interest, will be greater in the end.

Part I

SELF-ASSESSMENT

1

Is that *All* I Want to Believe?

'Exceed your expectations, even your own'
~ unknown

We all have pre-conceived notions of the present and future. Our pre-conception may be what we believe, but is it what we could *like* to believe about ourselves?

Are you really satisfied with where you are now and where everyone, including yourself, believes you will end as your final destination – as far as your job, home, friends and financial situation are concerned. This is what I am referring to when I say what "I want to believe." Where do you really want to be without the weight of where you are today? I don't care if you live in a ghetto or a million-dollar home. Let's dream and figure out what would truly be your definition of unrestricted success—that is, breakthrough success.

The first step when we are dreaming about our future is to take a full assessment of the present. What picture do we see of ourselves? What are the major dimensions of family life—house, job or career, vacations, and so on—that we want to assess? And more important, do we *believe* in that picture of ourselves?

Many people *think* they know where they want to go in life but have no idea even where they are today. How can you grow as a person if you're not aware you have a problem or know a better way to lead your life? To know and better understand where we think we are today, we must also must know how we got there.

We usually develop dreams and goals about what we desire in life while attending college or before starting our first job. But even if we've developed a dream in the past, it is often based on little, missing or biased information—or a combination of all three. We need to learn, as best as we can, what are the factors that have influenced who we are today. How have they made us think and view ourselves? We all have preconceived notions of the present and future. Our preconception may be what we believe, but is it what we would *like* to believe about ourselves? Who amongst us doesn't want more for themselves or their family?

As I mentioned earlier, in relating some of my own story, there are many past influences and influencers that bias perceptions of our current selves. In part, we're all biased, simply because we're too close to our own situation to be truly objective. But we're also subject to the projected biases placed on us by others, whether they be friends, family or associates. What they believe we are capable of accomplishing is affected by the history of their experiences with us as well as their own beliefs in themselves. After all, the people closest to us are those who most often have seen our many mistakes as well as their own. And, while our mistakes are a natural part of growing up— we make progress by making lots of mistakes while learning new things. Unfortunately, the people nearest to us see many more of these mistakes and remember them, as well as the discomforts or tragedies that come with them.

The biases of others, based on their own values and perception of our abilities, frequently limit our ability to achieve our potential. (This doesn't even include the less honorable feelings they might have, such as jealousy which we will deal with in a later chapter.) As a result, the perceptions many people have of themselves are lower than they should be, although there are exceptions, of course—people with inflated egos.

For inflated egos, one only has to look at a few politicians, a couple of actors or actresses and some star athletes to see examples of people whose opinions of themselves are way beyond reality. These people may suffer from advisers or colleagues who want to gain favor and are afraid to tell them exactly what they think or are concerned they may hurt someone's feelings.

I've seen a lot of interactions in the corporate world where people's fears of saying what they thought led to executives getting biased input. Some of the more insightful ones were able to see through this phenomenon—and appreciated efforts I made to cut through such biases. When I was at General Motors, for instance, my executive director, Gene Steininger, would often say to me, "I spent 32 years at General Motors and finally somebody tells me what they think rather than what they think I want to hear."

In another situation, when I first met the iconic Chrysler CEO, Lee Iacocca, he responded in a similar way. That day, he had been extremely busy and I was informed that he was in a terrible mood. In spite of this, I told Iacocca that I would give him my straight opinion, whether I thought he would like it or not. He made almost the identical statement to me that Gene Steininger made. My meeting with him was supposed to last only five minutes, as an introduction. He had two other meetings scheduled and was supposed to fly out in an hour and a half. Instead, our meeting lasted an hour and 35 minutes and his two other meetings were canceled. (I'm sure they had no trouble holding the corporate jet for him.)

We exchanged a lot of ideas. He was very receptive, not the hot-headed person people warned me about. The Lee Iacocca I met was an extremely intelligent man, focused on inspiring his company and starving for honest, well-thought-out recommendations. I understood him; I, too, get exasperated when people dance around a topic and can't, or won't, open up. If I hire someone, I expect them to have an opinion, support it or explain where they are stuck.

If we look deeper and broader, we can differentiate other traits that may affect our self-perceptions. We may see ourselves as highly skilled or weakly skilled. But our perceived weaknesses may be nothing more than unfulfilled or uneducated attempts to achieve something. Maybe you could've learned to sing, for example, but would never be sufficiently good to make it your career. Not everyone can do anything in spite of people saying to follow your passion. There are physical and mental limitations we all have as we grow. Early on, we will fluctuate between confidence, overconfidence and uncertainty, but we can work to utilize what we have—and most people are never aware of their potential in many areas.

I also have found interesting differences in self-perception between women and men. Women seem to be much more self-critical about appearance than they should be. For example, it seems that when a woman has some minor blemish in an insignificant part of her body, say her neck, it almost seems devastating. Men more often act as if they don't own a mirror. Sure, they may see their clothes and hair, but that is only the wrapper. In fact, you often find guys totally oblivious of their true appearance, walking around in a gym as if they're ripped bodybuilders, while they actually have big bellies or other signs of being drastically out of shape.

Besides being aware of biases in perception, it is important to know what we are missing—that is, skills and experiences we do or don't have.

For example, we may think we are or are not good in math or English, but there may be mitigating factors that make us think that. Is it really an innate weakness or deficiency or is it just the result of an approach we have been taught to learn these subjects? Were we influenced by perceptions of others or our own experiences entirely? There may be technical skills or social skills that we don't even know really are important in the eyes of people we want to accept us.

It may sound a bit odd to talk about knowing what you *don't* know. But we are really talking about many issues: weaknesses, missing information and further education. In the intelligence industry, it is said that it is not what you know that is important, but what you know that your enemy or opponent doesn't know that you know. The rationale is that your opponent or enemy can defend or guard against something when they are aware of it. But they won't if they don't even know something exists.

How does it relate to everyday life?

Knowledge and experience can come from 1) areas you understand; 2) areas you believe are currently your weaknesses; and 3) those that you are not even aware exist at this point in time. If you know your weaknesses and what you don't know—the missing pieces of your education—these can be learned; you can build skills and address them. Even those areas you aren't aware of at present, probably will become apparent as you make changes and expand your knowledge and experience. This is an ongoing process, something better understood when we look back at our more youthful years.

I often hear that young people today have no idea where they want to go. Certainly, when I was growing up, even in high school, we only knew reading, writing, science, math, history and languages as fields of interest. Sure, we knew a few careers as we watched TV or listened to people. But most had no idea the breadth of where education might lead us. We certainly didn't know most of the careers that any of these general fields could lead.

Those that went to college would usually spend the first two years in something general while learning what their major might be. Even after choosing and entering a major, we still didn't really know what careers were available to us.

With so much influence working against us and lack of knowledge about the missing pieces to our personal puzzle, it is little wonder most people never move out of their current trajectory. Many perceptions we have of ourselves are too high or too low, and any deviation from reality can have the effect of hampering our progress. These perceptions can limit ourselves or lead to major disappointments. Given that perceptions are generally not accurate, we can and should really concentrate on what we want to be or have in life and seek out an understanding what it takes to get there.

When we start on a journey, we have a destination in mind. When increasing our skills and abilities, we may have a goal in mind. While we may be aware of a path to achieve the goal, as we learn more and increase our skill set, the goal we have, as well as the path to that goal may well change. We should expect to aim higher and aim for outcomes we consider better. As we grow and learn, we must realize that we learn more about ourselves.

One key to success is embracing this process of discovery in this never-ending journey. We need to be ready for opportunities, we see as we learn, both in formal education as well as in what life's experiences present to us.

Whatever our goals, they may change as we learn about new potential goals. During this time of change, our values, desires and preferences change, too. Furthermore, what we're willing to do today to attain a goal may be completely different with new experiences and with new confidence. No matter what our age, we should realize that we can always reassess our current lifestyle and goals.

Throughout this book we will examine how we change, develop new habits, gain confidence and advance ourselves, not just in terms of goals, but how we grow, and grow beyond our or other people's expectations.

I do not want to deliver an assessment tool. I really want you to dream, to take the perceptions you have of yourself, question them and reshape them to what you *want* to believe as your dream. Hopefully, that will lead you to new and exciting places. As you grow, misperceptions and biases will start to fall away and new doorways and goals will come into view.

How will we find out whether our perceptions are accurate or not? Will we even need to do that? If we decide life is a journey and constantly can be improved, perceptions we have of ourselves and our abilities, both good and bad, will be revealed and will change over time. Our only goal is to head them in a positive, enriching direction.

2

Oh My God, You're a Parent!

*'If you have never been hated by your child,
you have never been a parent'*
~ Bette Davis

Becoming a parent may be one of the best ways to illustrate how we learn new things and adapt to change in our lives. Everyone understands the trials and tribulations parents go through. Even if you don't have kids, you can appreciate the rough times, lack of sleep, constant interruptions and responsibilities. You may not truly understand the depth of their exhaustion, but you certainly understand their difficulties. Oh my God, you're parents—good luck with that!

Why am I discussing parenthood in a book on success? Well, when we look at our children and realize how much they must learn as they grow, and then consider what we adults don't know and still must learn as adults—and what we can actually learn from our children—it really helps put life in perspective. Whether you're raising children or expanding your friendships in order to expand your life, you need to understand how others learn.

We all see the astonishing speed that babies learn. But it's important to note that parents are continually learning, too. Beyond learning how to care *for* a child, they learn *from* the child through daily experience and responsibility.

A little divergence here may be useful here to understand how off-target all of us might be at times in our pursuit of success. To understand what you need, you need to think of others, their goals and how they reached those goals. This applies to everyone, from a child to a customer, and includes everything from their self-perception to relationship-building and satisfaction with one's life.

Why is this important?

Because when we think of ourselves, we naturally are going to be biased in our assessment of what's important and what's needed. What's important to *the other person,* whether they're a child or a customer? How do *they* feel? Not only what they *think* is important, but what they actually need. Think of both the child and the new parent: They have zero experience and little idea what to expect in the future. In this way, how people raise their children from birth to adulthood can also serve as an example how we, as adults, raise ourselves through adulthood. Think about what we're doing now, then back to what our childhood was like.

What are the truly important goals we, as parents, should be setting for our children? I don't believe they're what most people think they are. So, if we're not properly setting the goals, expectations and paths for our own children, how are we going to do it for ourselves? Let's look at that, since we have a better chance viewing how we raise our children with less bias than in viewing our own self-assessment.

For new parents, especially, the job of parenting can be overwhelming, not only the obvious maintenance chores, but coaching, encouragement, tutoring and mentoring. Why, then, do parents say, "I am going to give my kids all those things I never had"?

When I hear that sentence, a little devil appears in my head. I have done exactly the following many times, publicly.

"That's great!" I say. "You are teaching them *all* the life skills they need to grow up–in fact, all skills *you* learned while growing up. That is really great." Now you can imagine the dumbfounded look on their face. I know that's not what they meant, but I want to wake them up. It may be the little devil in me, but I truly want people to realize that they have the life of their child in their hands.

Of course, they usually respond, feebly, saying "No. I mean the things that I couldn't afford to buy when I was growing up. I want them to have those things that my parents couldn't afford."

But is that goal really in the spirit of what's best for the child? Ultimately, parents are giving immediate satisfaction without any consideration of the implications on the child's future. Perhaps this is as much for their own ego gratification as for the smile on the child's face. Frankly, I don't care what their reasoning is; I do care about the effect on the child.

By now you probably can see the parallel: The scenario of adults trying to satisfy their children the same way they satisfy themselves, obtaining things they want now, rather than investing in their future. If an individual is fully aware of the sacrifice they are making from their future to fulfill current satisfaction, well then, okay. That's their choice.

But later, if someone whines about life being "unfair" or that they don't have something they now realize they need, you have to wonder how much they prepared for their current state. I'm reminded of the expression, "If you fail to plan, you plan to fail." But we are not simply talking about your own short- term versus long-term gratification here. We are talking about the effect on your child and the responsibility to that child's upbringing. We are building "traits and habits" for the child, just as we should for ourselves, if we want to achieve what we call success.

To understand this more fully, I believe we can learn not only from other people; we can take lessons from nature.

For example, why aren't we as smart as some of the animals in the forest? On some level, humans don't even seem to be as astute as birds. Birds routinely prepare their young to leave the nest and go out on their own. We, the "intelligent" species, don't necessarily do the same preparation—or at least not with the thorough commitment of a bird. Now, *that* is ironic. We think of birds as dumb, "bird-brains." Maybe they're just acting on some genetic impulse that reveals itself as good parenting. If so, have we intellectualized our own parenting to suppress the very same trait?

It's one thing to see a parent want to give their kids some new toy or technology; it is another to see what appears to be a contest among parents of who can give their kids the most things. Are we too often focused on satisfying our kids' pleadings? Are we focusing on our self-images, our own satisfaction, personal feelings and accomplishments? And finally, are we unwilling to be "parents" and more interested in being a "friend" to our kids?

It is true that teaching your children to handle life is a far more difficult task than buying a few items because some other kid has it or our own kid sees a commercial and wants it. But now, I'm asking you to reflect on the importance of being a parent, a continuous evaluator, motivator and teacher. How are you going to do this for yourself without constant excuses if you can't do it for the very child you cherish?

The desire to satisfy a child's yearning for a toy is the same as our own desire for some new adult toy. We need to focus on the longer-term benefit or skill that we are equipping the child to be on its own later in life.
Damn, if birds can do it, why can't we?

The ability to learn and grow—a skill we need to teach our children—is also something we need to learn and correct in ourselves. Granted, it's difficult to postpone current satisfaction and decide instead to work, study or educate yourself. Whether acting as a parent or working on our own growth, we must postpone current gratification to make progress. And whether for a child or ourselves, we must be able to have the discipline and strength to carry out the task.

Still, since the process of discovering new ideas and opportunities will never end, we need to enjoy this very long journey, as difficult as it may be, and love the progress we make in life. Just as we might support a child with encouragement and guidance, we must seek out the right influences and do the same for ourselves. As adults, many of us stop growing, either because of a decision we make, a decision someone else makes for us, or the influence of others.

Why stop?

Life *should* be an enjoyable journey. Seek out the stimuli and the encouragement you need to make it so. Surround yourself with other people who want to grow and learn.

3

Passion Can Suck...the Life Out of You

'Passion is 80% Attitude!'
~ Thomas O'Grady, PhD

These days, you hear everybody—especially entrepreneurs—talking about passion: "Follow your passion and success will follow." You are expected to become a new entrepreneur just by following the things you love to do. After all, since you are passionate about your dream, you will overcome all obstacles—or so the proclamations imply. Well, it's not that easy. There are two sides to passion. You may be passionate about something, but passion is also something you *develop* from attitude and the experience of success.

I've got a clue for you: Passion can suck the life out of you. What do I mean by that? First, let's acknowledge that it's wonderful to have a love for what you're doing (more later on about how you can develop that desire), but it's no mantra that if you follow your passion and put your money on your passion, success will follow. It's not some magical law of attraction. There's a little bit of truth to the idea that if you have the right enthusiasm and emit a wonderful positive attitude, people will feel more comfortable around you and you're more likely to get customers. But passion alone will not guarantee customers flocking to your door.

Before you plow your passion into any entrepreneurial venture, ask yourself some direct and practical questions: Does it actually pay well? Are there economies of scale, or are you just going to be trading your hours for the same amount of money? (If so, it's just another job.) Is there room for increased productivity? The passion for your hobby—let's say scrapbooking or stamp collecting—may feel very different when you turn it into a business and all of a sudden you realize you have to do marketing, sales and bookkeeping, manage employees, satisfy vendors, suppliers, and comply with government regulations. Is this still the thing you loved? It is no longer just a passion; it's something much more complex, much more difficult. In fact, what entrepreneurs often find is that many of the less desirable parts of the business are those that others either don't want to do or don't do well. If you're going push on past your passion, you must be ready for these contingencies.

Next, analyze whether there is really a market for your entrepreneurial product or service. Motivational speakers and marketers love to pedal the idea of following your passion, but if you can't sell your passion to consumers, it won't help you. You have to fill some need or demand that someone is willing to pay for. Can you completely fill that need?

The next time you're at a shopping center or driving by a strip mall, take a look at all the empty stores. Most likely, those former store owners had a passion for what they were doing, but they still failed. They probably had to guarantee their loans with the bank or other creditors with everything they had—their home, their savings, everything. You can be sure that they stretched out their cash and went into debt, trying to make their business work right up until the end. Their passion simply wasn't enough.

You have to make sure that you have a combination of the right skills to create a product that will fill sufficient demand, and that the market isn't over-supplied. If something is so desirable or fun that many people crowd into the field, it probably won't pay enough to earn you sufficient income. But that doesn't necessarily mean you have to go into the market niche with the highest income. If something is satisfying to you, you may develop great pride in it and feel fulfilled. But you must have realistic expectations. Most often, acquiring wealth for your future is more about how you use your money, not necessarily how much you earn.

Ask yourself: What are my goals? What are the desires I have? If you're interested in just earning a few hundred extra dollars a month and you're going to put aside that money for your retirement, fine. But if your venture will not realize the money you truly desire, either accept the situation and enjoy what you are doing or move on to something else. You might consider other means of saving for your future, either by reducing your expenses or getting other kinds of side work. Whatever your decision, the key is to accept responsibility for the results. Don't spoil your success with petty jealousy of others and the complaint that life is "unfair."

Now, let's take a closer look at one of the most coveted entrepreneurial passions: opening your own restaurant. Actually, it is the worst of all businesses—very, very few survive. Even if you do survive, you will have to put in ridiculously arduous hours. You have to be up early to buy fresh produce or meat, then get things set up for the day, and finally, end up staying late at night to close out the myriad tasks and operational details. If anything happens to a cook, manager or other staff member, you may have to work extra on days off or on the weekends, just trying to get everything done. And, that doesn't account for the other functions I mentioned earlier, such as bookkeeping and complying with government regulations.

A few years ago, I thought about fulfilling my own culinary passion by opening a bakery café. I didn't expect to make much money, just to do it as a retirement diversion. I would have 10 or 12 tables, make some money, but also have the ability to put up a sign once in a while: "Gone skiing. See you tomorrow."

Then one day I bumped into Tom Douglas at an airport in Philadelphia. Douglas is a very successful restaurateur who owns about 20 restaurants in the Seattle area and also provides or designs the meals served on Alaska Airlines. I started chatting with him about my café concept. "Gee, it's really hard," he said. Douglas didn't even know that as a kid, I had worked in restaurants as a busboy and a waiter and even had to work in the kitchen a few times and more recently just finished attending the Culinary Institute of America for baking and pastry, so I knew what it was like. But he added: "So many people want to do that. What I do is offer them—and if you want to come in, you can do it—I offer them to come into my workplace for a week. After a week, they're saying, 'Oh my God.' They realize the complexity, the work, and everything else that's involved, and all of a sudden their passion disappears." Passion is far from enough in this most desired business.

That says a lot about the notion of "following your passion." Make certain that you really know what is involved in your passion. While restaurants are the most desired start-up businesses, they also require massive obligations from their would-be entrepreneurs, and more than any other business, they fail. I still might open my cafe someday, but meanwhile, my neighbors love the desserts I learned to make at the Culinary Institute.

There are lots of artistic passions you might want to pursue as a career: Becoming a writer, a painter (I'm not talking about house painters), as well as singers, musicians, actors, actresses. Those are all passions. Will you make money at it? Maybe. There are some people who do extremely well, but it's rare. If you have that substantial talent, great. But to think that passion alone will get your talent through seems too simple. There are other complicating factors such as the number of people already in the field, what the demand is for these positions, and what the likelihood is of really making it, given that in many of these "spots" or opportunities in these worlds are slotted for family or close friends. I have a good friend who is a fine musician who performs as a 'first' with a couple of symphonies. He loves it and has a lot of passion for it, but he earns his "real" money working at a major software company.

In reality, most passions don't map into great careers. When people are asked about their current job, only 21% of them say they like it. There are a number of reasons for that. One is that there are a bunch of unhappy people out there, period, that's just the way they are. I meet them every day, you meet them every day. There are others who choose jobs or careers for their own personal or pragmatic reasons. There are still others, who would just like to go to work every day, make some money, then go home; they only want to work 9 to 5 and don't care about ever getting ahead. That's fine. That's their choice. Then there are those of us who do have a passion and desire to do something more and keep in mind what it's about.

Whatever you choose for your career or business, it is a personal choice. At the beginning of this book, I set out clearly that as an economist, I view a person's definition of success as theirs alone, and neither I nor anyone else else can evaluate it versus our own. There is, however, one qualification. This assumes that you make that decision with good knowledge of the consequences and full understanding of the choices. My intent is to assist with the decision, not make it.

As an example of the potential dilemma in making such choices, let's examine the question: How should a person decide to pursue their success when they are young? As a middle-aged adult, I used to go skiing usually in the mornings three times a week—I'm only an hour and 15 minutes from the ski slopes. Fairly often, somebody who was either a ski instructor or part of the ski patrol would be on the lift with me, and we'd be chatting. They were, of course, very passionate about skiing.

I use this to draw a comparison between what I did when I was young and what he chose. I spent my younger years gaining experience, credentials, all the things that helped propel me into doing a lot of really rewarding things. They were spending their younger years enjoying things: skiing in the winter, scuba diving in summer or flying to the Southern Hemisphere to ski there.

Which decision is right? I can't say. What I *would* say to this young person is, "That's great. It's really neat you are doing things like this, and for the rest of your life you'll have those memories." It's too late for me to do the type of skiing he's doing. I could never do that now. On the other hand, I have higher income, more assets, probably more long-term security and more choices I can make now. That's what I have, but he has memories of experiences I can never experience now.

Interesting....Which is the right thing to do? When a ski instructor is younger, strong and able, and he has a lifestyle flexible enough to do those things, why not? True, when he gets older he might not live in a house that's as nice as mine, but he should understand the outcomes of the choices he made and not be jealous. That's the key. He had the passion; that was wonderful. He did exciting things that I never was able to do nor will ever do. There is no right choice. It's an individual preference—that's my economic lesson for the day.

There are also lots of other jobs that may fulfill the needs of younger people, without necessarily fulfilling their passions or long-term goals. For example: tasks like caring for family dogs and cats, teaching positions or service jobs like flight attendants. I fly a lot on Alaska Airlines, and had many interactions with flight attendants on most airlines over the years. The flight attendants on Alaska Airlines are wonderful, really nice, always polite. Interestingly, at a number of other airlines, many attendants seem resentful because they haven't gotten big pay raises. (How could they? Is the airline able to make more money because they're being more productive? No.) At Alaska Airlines, however, flight attendants acknowledge that the job they're doing is generally for younger people. They're basically saying things like: "Well, this is a nice job with a lot of benefits, but it's not a long-term career to make a lot of money and put aside." These flight attendants, really do have a passion for what they're doing, but they also understand what the limitations of that position are. Following your passion may not be viable over the long term, but you can still develop your passion—just like those flight attendants.

How, then, can you actually develop your passion? A lot of it stems from attitude. When I was younger, for example, I worked at some pretty low-end jobs: a caddy on golf courses; a busboy, then waiter; and a proof boy (I'll explain that one in a minute). When I was working as a waiter, most people would say to me: "That's a hard job. You're doing all kinds of thing, trying to make people happy." But I looked at it as an opportunity: While I was there, I had the ability to make each couple's evening something truly special. That helped satisfy and create my passion. And guess what? I made much more in tips than almost every other waiter or waitress. Why? Because the customers were happier; they saw my desire to give them a great evening.

As a proof boy in a big union print shop I literally made the proofs for new ads and pages and brought them over to the editors. Everything was nice and neat around me. I kept the proofs timely. I was happy doing that job. Even though I knew it was a temporary job—it was during the summer before college—I found ways to be proud of what I did. I learned that you can develop a passion based on attitude, a pride in what you accomplished.

The best example I ever saw of this kind of attitude was in New York City, where I used to go on a regular basis to train software developers. I stayed at a hotel in lower Manhattan and one time I went downstairs to get some coffee that the company had set up for everybody. There happened to be three sanitation workers there, and we had a conversation I didn't expect. "Boy, wait until you get back here tonight," they told all of us in the lobby. "You will not find a piece of paper or garbage anywhere around. The outside in all of this neighborhood will be so clean you won't see a scrap of paper." Did they have a passion for their job? Absolutely. I respected them. They loved doing their job well; it gave them a great deal of satisfaction. They showed me how important is was not to simply look at a job. Passion is not what you do, but how you do it—you can develop pride in any job.

In short, there's a lot more to turning your passion into entrepreneurial success than just launching with passion and setting up a store or getting on the Internet. Yes, you can have a hobby and make some money, maybe only a few hundred dollars, maybe a lot more. But to be truly successful, there's much more to it. You have to have an overall strategy, including an understanding of what your product really offers; how to put together the right tools and skills; and create the right marketing plan. And instead of relying on innate passion, you might learn how to find that passion through the attitudes you develop from life experiences.

So the next time you hear somebody say, "Follow your passion," think, "With what?"

4

Are You Able?

'Look in the Mirror, that is your Competition!'
~ unknown

How many times do we hear people say, "I can't" or "It can't be done?"

I truly believe in the expression, "You don't know until you try it," and even then, you probably don't really know. Why? If you try something without a belief that you will succeed, you're already preparing yourself to accommodate failure. In your mind, you are putting into play a safety mechanism to accept failure, rather than accommodate success. Most people avoid disappointments, and in the process, avoid trying. But isn't every learning experience a series of trials and errors, of successes and disappointments?

Part of preparing to take on new things and succeed at higher and higher levels is to learn to love the journey—the very process of change. When you enter new territory, you'll inevitably hit a lot of rough spots. Think of your journey as a game or sport. Try several things, and even if only one or two succeed, you should celebrate the successes. Consider the baseball player who doesn't get a hit 2 out of 3 times at bat fails two-thirds of the time—but ends up in the Hall of Fame!

Using a game approach to learning is something that can be applied to many sectors of life. It reminds me of the time I was standing in front of a group of software developers, ready to teach them some programming skills. Many of them would be playing games on their computer, usually solitaire, even during the presentation. I told them I couldn't understand why people played those computer games. It seemed quite silly to me that a bunch of people trying to become better professionals were playing games to kill time rather than making a game out of what they needed to learn.

There were "programming objects" on the computer system that they needed to learn, and trying to figure them out could be a game. Not like solitaire, where you probably don't remember how many games you won and lost—or even how many games you played—the day after you played. But if you treated those little programming objects like games and tried to figure them out, you could not only win, but make progress. A minor explanation. When you click on something on a computer, you see something happen. If you right click, you can usually see several things that can be done. All of those are programmed. When new software is released, these programmers need to learn how to use potential actions or properties to benefit users. So, playing with these instead of a mindless game, you would learn something. And even if you didn't figure it out today, you would get to play again tomorrow.

Isn't this the way most people are in life? They play games for hours, with all kinds of claims that they "need down time," then they complain that they "have no time." The key is attitude. Make your project—and all of its pieces—a game.

An important part of changing behavior is moving your mental attitude from "I can't" to "How do I? Or "What is necessary for me to be successful?" I addressed this directly at one of the companies I previously owned, by forbidding the use of the words "can't" or "cannot." While that might sound extreme (and most employees thought it was), what I wanted from people was for them to think of their tasks as mathematical problems or maybe even home improvement projects. That is, what did they know, and what information was missing—or what piece of the problem couldn't they solve? The missing pieces were the things that still needed to be solved or be handled with a workaround. While one particular person might not know how to complete something, someone else might know an answer to one of the missing pieces. That is exactly how progress is made in mathematics and science.

However, as soon as a person says, "I can't," their search for an answer has ended. The same is true when looking at our future. It is what we *can* do right now that matters, not what we *can't* do. Even if we can't fully solve the problem, at least we can make some contribution, some movement, toward a solution—and then we (or someone else) will be able to concentrate only on the unknown parts, without distractions.

We constantly hear how we are getting closer and closer to a cure for certain types of cancer or diabetes. Well, how is that done? Can you imagine, if the researchers who hadn't found a cure yet just concluded that they couldn't? Just as cures in science or solutions in mathematics are achieved in increments over time—with small successes and many attempts—such is the case with our life. All big problems are best viewed in little pieces and best understood one step at a time. If we work on a problem and solve only 50 percent of it, well, we're still better off, right? We're farther down the road toward a solution, and the next time we tackle this challenge, we may be able to move yet another few steps closer toward an ideal solution. We need to look at life as a journey, not a single effort. Even if that is as far as we get, 50 percent, wouldn't our estimates be better.

No matter how we set our goals, there is a price to pay in time and effort to achieve what we want to be. We realize, for example, that no professional athlete gets to high levels of achievement without pushing themselves to extremes. The same is true for Nobel Prize winners. I saw this first-hand when I got to graduate school. Initially, I only marveled at how brilliant that these Nobel Laureate professors were. But when I saw how dedicated and hard-working each one was, a whole new view of them came to me.

One of my early lessons in how much effort it took to raise your goals to a higher level occurred when I was about 19 years of age. At the time, my best friend was a champion power lifter. I was a skinny kid and was having some trouble with my knees. My friend said he would help me build up my muscles, which would strengthen my legs and knees. Well, in only three months and one week, by listening and doing exactly what he said, I gained 32 pounds of muscle. (Even to this day, I've yet to see anyone else attain these results.) Before my friend offered to train me, I tried to exercise and made gains unsuccessfully. But he was my coach and I had faith in him, which actually wasn't that hard, since he was a true champion. He won the Oklahoma, New Mexico, Texas tri-state heavyweight championship.

At the time, I never dreamed that I could have had so much success, but had the privilege of having a friend I respected and never questioned. He had the credentials. I believed in his wisdom. My part was simply putting in the effort. Now of course, I don't want to downplay the effort. I had many people come up to me and ask me to show them what I did. I gladly did, but unfortunately, those who took me up on the offer promptly quit. It was too hard. Do you want success and are you willing to put in the work?

How many people do you know that fit into that same category? The key components of my success were: I had a mentor whose wisdom I respected; I was willing to do exactly as I was told, listening to thorough explanations without challenging his direction; and I accepted the idea that I could gain muscle despite having failed previously, and repeatedly.

Much of people's success or mediocrity in academics can also be attributed to effort or lack thereof. In my case, I learned in the military that I could push my body and mind much further than I thought I could, and this lesson served me well when I entered college. Before starting school, I decided that I would give up my social life for 2½ years in order to maximize my grades. Why 2½ years? I realized that whatever graduate school or law school I might choose, my acceptance would be determined by the grades I got during that time frame. While 2½ years sounds like an incredibly long time, there were two things in my mind. First, the military put my life on hold for 4 years, so I knew it could be done. Second, I put in perspective that this 2½-year period was an investment into possibly the next 50+ years of life. This time would be highly concentrated study and work toward attaining the best grades and records possible.

I knew my academic record would be important to get into the best school possible to gain entry into the highest possible set of opportunities. The best possible graduate school would give me access to the best faculty and the best fellow students. That atmosphere would help make me better, and ultimately give me lifelong credibility and access and to people and jobs. I didn't know exactly where I was going or which specific career path I would take to get there. But I did know that whatever I chose, it would be important to get access to the best faculty mentors in order to learn the most. And even though I had no idea what I was able to do, I did know—most importantly—how to push my body and my mind, thanks to both my experiences with the military and weightlifting.

Still, if a person only dreams of doing what they know how to do or what they *think* they can do, then they have already limited themselves. That is, they're allowing their current environment and experience to limit their dreams before they can even understand what is feasible or available to them—or whether it would be worthwhile.

What if you change your mind while heading toward a goal? After all, you're learning new things about yourself, developing new skills which open up to new opportunities, possibilities and potential successes. So it's quite reasonable for you to change your mind.

If you have a very specific dream, and along the way to that dream you decide to stop or go on a different path, you'll still be much further along on your journey than if they only took what came your way, without stretching out to learn new things. Also, if you don't push yourself to reach some dreamier goal, you might never discover those new options and the people available to help you. And you may never develop the qualifications you need to achieve such goals.

The first key decision is to choose a dream as a *target*. Create the life you want by taking one step at a time. Later, you can worry about taking action, but for now breaking down that dream into steps can bring it into a sequence of realistic targets. This is your dream, not what someone else wants or expects of you. It is what *you* think will make you happy and successful.

It is not just current skills and experiences that determine our life's path. The process of learning what we want and finding out what is necessary to achieve those goals gives us clues about new skills that we may need to develop, leading to new possibilities, skills, and potentially more choices—an explosion of opportunities. Yes, the more you learn and the better you develop your skills, the more varied the opportunities that will open up.

What you learn improves your ability to navigate any new or existing path and usually makes it easier. You are not only expanding your knowledge, but becoming accustomed to change, and developing a new attitude toward change itself. Keep your eye on the ball. Remember, if you get a hit 1 out of every 3 times you're up at the plate, you are a superstar.

Increasing your skills and knowledge also will help boost your commitment to whatever you choose; that is, you are doing something by choice, not default. Furthermore, it will reduce disappointments and the "I shouldas, wouldas and couldas." Later in life, nobody wants to look back and realize there were so many things they could have done to make their life better. Nobody wants to get to their later years and say, "If only I did this," or "I could have been just like him or her." There are always choices—some of which will be good and some of which will be bad—but you never want to have to say, "I didn't try."

It is interesting that just recently someone asked me, do you regret anything you did in life and wish you had taken a different path. I thought for a moment and said, no. It was a great question and while I gave up some opportunities, some very big, I can honestly say that I have no regrets.

5

Know Your Weaknesses—and 'Go on a Diet'

'It isn't the mountains ahead to climb that pull you down, it's the pebble in your shoe'
~ Muhammad Ali

How often it is said, "Do what you are good at"? In this age of extreme specialization, it is commonplace to tell people to concentrate on their strengths—you might become exceptional in those skills—and ignore your weaknesses.

Contrary to popular belief in most circles, you shouldn't work only on your strengths. That is, while you are concentrating entirely on strengths, weaknesses will often pull you down, limit your success and limit the usability of the skills you do have. You probably won't be able to eliminate those weaknesses altogether, but you may find a way to go on a "diet" and shed some of the weaknesses weighing you down.

Too much emphasis is placed on finding what your best skills are. There are batteries of tests that may help you determine what you should be, but take them simply as tests of your skill-level; don't let yourself be limited by them. A lot of life requires you to be somewhat broader, not an expert in everything, but better or at least adequate in many areas beyond your primary interest.

First, take inventory of your strengths and weaknesses, as well as the skills that are both necessary and useful for your career. You probably still need certain skills that you may not be good at just yet that might be considered weaknesses. In general, we may say that careers have a series of dependencies, not just a skill or two—or as we often say in statistics, things are highly correlated.

One example of a skill that I didn't have in my past—but ultimately couldn't accept as a weakness—was public speaking. This is something that scares most people. I have often heard that the only fear greater than speaking in front of people is being in a fire. But where would I be today if I didn't learn how to speak in public? Speaking is an essential skill for successful people in many occupations, indeed, an important skill for many areas of life.

I can vividly recall the time I was finishing graduate school at Berkeley and flew around the country on the interview circuit. I remember one incident, in particular. There I was in front of two professors who were looking to hire me. They asked me some simple questions—so simple, in fact, that I doubted my own hearing and I froze, distracted by random thoughts. And this wasn't the first time that I had problems with speaking. It didn't matter whether I was presenting a book report or speaking in front of a whole room. It was a fear I always had. Even when I was in the military, responsible for critical analysis of Soviet intelligence, I was expected to present to high-ranking officers—and it was always such a horrible experience; I was literally shaking.

Fortunately, in the course of a very brief period, I was able to overcome my fear of speaking—with outside help and a safe, secure environment for me to learn this skill. Clearly, this weakness was limiting my opportunities, as it limited the potential of many others, and it was well worth my effort to overcome it. Now, speaking in public is actually one of my strengths.

To show how easy it was to overcome, let me explain what I discovered and how that discovery made a huge shift in my understanding of learning. When I got my first job after graduate school, I wanted to start fresh, so I sought out ways to become more comfortable, or at least more confident. I tried all kinds of mind tricks, attempting to gain confidence, but none of them were working.

Then I took the Dale Carnegie course on public speaking. As with most people, I had visions of speaking in public or being the 'life of the party' or gathering, but the fear is really about embarrassing myself. Now, it was not just a matter of taking the course, but what I did, in particular, during the course that set the stage for success. As I was listening to the introduction— how we would be speaking in front of the group at least a couple of times every evening—all my usual fears started to surface. And I didn't know any of these people. Initially, this made me even more nervous, since they all knew others in the class and had a kind of support group of friends. Then I thought to myself, "I will probably never see any of them ever again. What, then, do I have to fear? Why should I care how foolish I might look?"

At that point, I realized that I was spending my money to learn how to speak and here was an instructor who was an expert. I decided that I would do exactly what I was asked to do, regardless of how idiotic I thought it might be or how idiotic I might look. This place would become my personal laboratory, a safe environment to experiment and jump out of my comfort zone. If the instructor wanted me to crawl like a snake or quack like a duck, why not try to do the best crawl or quack I could? Embarrassment became irrelevant.

As I sat through the rest of the introduction, I heard the instructors describe how they would award mechanical pencils as prizes multiple times per night to people during each class. Nobody could win the same award more than once. I felt that maybe one night I might be able to win the "Most Improved Award" for the week. Eventually, I figured, when many others had already won that award and since I was starting at such an abysmal state, I might be one of those that after the better people won it I might get it. Hopefully, since I was coming from such a dismal place in public speaking and confidence, my improvement should show. Certainly, I was not going to be top in anything else.

So there I sat, knowing that I would let myself go and do whatever was asked with complete commitment. I would do my best. My fears were mostly gone. I just continually reminded myself that I didn't know these people. They would never see me again, and I didn't care what they thought of me.

Early on, there was an assignment where we had to imitate something in the house, as if we were that object or piece of equipment. I chose a garbage disposal. I went up there and enjoyed being a garbage disposal, getting stuck, being afraid as a broom came down to clear me and get running again. In my mind, I visualized everything. That helped me loosen up. There were also impromptu speaking contests and a variety of other challenges.

Well, as it turned out, I never won that weekly Most Improved Award. I won every other award. In the final week, after I was voted the best overall speaker for the course, I gave an acceptance speech in which I told everyone what my background was; what my expectations were as I entered the course; and the overwhelming feeling I had as the course concluded. I had stretched myself way outside my comfort zone.

Unfortunately, since many of the students came with friends or made friends in the course, most of them probably pushed themselves only a little. I think it might be referred to as "pushing the envelope." I often noticed how they looked to each other for confidence and support. But they were actually holding themselves back, avoiding what they thought might be socially unacceptable or somewhat embarrassing and reluctant to jump too far outside their own comfort zone—or the comfort zone of their friends. It's not easy to push outside your comfort zone when you care about the opinions and expectations of others watching you. People may suggest, "Why not take a class with friends; you'll feel more comfortable learning together." Well, you've just limited your potential. Better to go alone.

That experience taught me a great deal about learning and the limiting influence of friends and the environment. At the time, I was well past the age when most people start to learn to speak in public, even if they had the ability or talent. The key for me was being in a safe environment where I could step out of my comfort zone, and having a good mentor or teacher. This was an important lesson for me, not just releasing myself to speak, but providing another reminder that I could overcome weaknesses, if I just worked at them in the right way and away from the influence of people who knew me.

Like public speaking, math is another area that people frequently claim as a "weakness," How many times have you heard somebody say they are "bad in math"? This is mostly a learned response, based on the way you've been taught and what other people tell you about yourself.

Why do I say this? First, the requirements today are far less stringent than 30 or 40 years ago. Back then, you had to learn the required math and pass certain tests, or else you would not graduate from one grade to the next. The ability of high school students isn't worse today; math just isn't required as much as in years past. Now whether you believe students should be forced to conform to these requirements is not the issue I'm discussing here. Rather, I'm saying the *ability* to pass all high school math is probably the same or at least as high as in the past, but the motivation and belief is not. It's rare, in my opinion, that a student can't learn high school math, and learn it well.

Nevertheless, many kids are taught that if they are good in English they are bad at math. (A Russian friend once asked me, "Why are Americans so proud of being bad at math?") And conversely, if you're good in math, you're supposed to be bad in English. I propose that the major difference between being good or bad at math is the teaching and the learning methods. To begin with, anyone who is good in English or history—or any subject that has a lot of reading, for that matter—is generally a fast reader. At least, they're fast compared to me. So what happens to them when they "read" math?

Here's a little secret I discovered, which I've subsequently shared with many students.

Even if a student is a "fast" reader, they're often not told how long they should expect to take in studying a single page of math. I bring them through a series of questions. I say to them, "You probably read a page in one or two minutes, right?" Yes, they answer. "So when you read a math book, you must get frustrated after reading for five or 10 minutes and you don't understand what you've just read?" Again, yes. These students are quickly overcome with self-doubt because they don't know that it requires much more time to think through rigorous math problems than it does to read paragraphs of normal English or history text. I explain to the students that I'm very good at math—I have a Ph.D. in mathematical and statistical economics—and yet I may need to spend 45 minutes to understand a single page of a complicated math book. If I spent only two or three minutes, I, too, might feel equally frustrated.

It comes down to expectations. What are the expectations of a fast reader? I explained this concept in one-on-one conversations with several high school students who claimed to be bad in math. When I revisited this problem with them a year later, I found it very interesting what happened after I changed their expectations about the time it took to study math. In each case, they told me they were now good in math. They didn't just say, "I'm doing well in math." They said, "I'm *very good* at math."

Not only can math be learned well, but it's important that it is learned well—for all of us. This issue popped up for me at a recent visit to Starbucks where, as usual, I decided to chat with people nearby. (More about that later.) A grandmother and her grandson were sitting across from me on the comfortable chairs. The grandson was very nice and I complimented him. In the conversation, I heard what grade he was attending and what the grandmother and he were doing in arithmetic over the summer. I mentioned how important it was that he learned well. Some people today, including some teachers, seem to believe that you can rely on calculators. Unfortunately, I don't see any of these teachers carrying around calculators and whipping them out everywhere. Hmmm....Where are those teachers shopping?

I then explained to the boy, why is it important to be quick in basic arithmetic. At times, I told him, you will need to know if you are not getting the right change back from a store purchase, or what somebody is telling you to make a point in a discussion about presidential polling numbers just doesn't make sense. You won't need to calculate; just the numbers you are hearing may not feel right. How do you develop the feeling when something just doesn't seem right? Well, if you understand the arithmetic in your head, you will intuitively have a sense when something just doesn't seem right. I gave him a little contest he could play by himself that would make him good at basic arithmetic. The boy and his grandmother thought it was easy, very cool.

It is incredible the things we feel are acceptable in basic skills. One, unfortunately, not unusual occurrence, is when you are getting change for a purchase. You hand a cashier a 10-dollar bill and 13 cents and they get lost. I was in a Verizon store and my data allotment was just increased from 10 to 12 gigabytes. I asked the clerk to look up to see what data allotment I had left this period. When he pulled it up, it said I used 8.25. I immediately said, thank you, good

I've got 3.75 gigabytes remaining. He said, wow, that's incredible how you figured that out. Really?

So again, it is critical that as you dream of what you want to be, you don't impose limits before you even try. And if you were to only focus on your strengths and avoid your weaknesses, you would be vastly limiting your opportunities before you even start to dream. Identify what skills you have and also those that you don't have or you might consider areas of weakness. There are many skills you can buy from other people. There are some that can or should be either learned or at least minimally understood.

When you evaluate your weaknesses, don't just think in terms of school subjects. There are many important skills including speaking, mathematics, communications, writing, stamina, persistence, time management and goal setting among others. Yes, stamina and persistence are skills, like the bird or the mother teaching their young, or the baby learning to walk. How many times have you heard someone say something "isn't working out for them"? How many months does that take for a baby to learn to walk? Can you imagine a baby looking up at its mother after a couple of days or weeks and saying, "I'm sorry, but this walking thing is just not working for me." Think of your weaknesses as temporary, something to overcome. Face your fears and work to overcome, or at least, reduce them.

Remember, it is not the difficulty of a skill that weeds us out from success. It is either our own self-selection (we're convinced we're no good) or it is the teaching methodology (the way we've been taught a skill) is faulty—or both. People sometimes marvel at my skill in Japanese and my former ability in Russian. But for years, I thought I was no good at learning languages, until I realized the problem was the way I was taught in school. Later, I was taught much more effective techniques, like learning new vocabulary by *thinking* in the foreign language, not translating words from English into that language.

To many who have tried to learn a language like Japanese, my acquired proficiency seems amazing. I have often heard, "Wow, to learn Japanese, you need to be extremely smart." I usually reply, "Actually, the dumbest person in Japan speaks Japanese."

6

Limits Are Often Self-imposed

'There are no limits to growth, because there are no limits on the human capacity for intelligence, imagination and wonder.'
~ Ronald Reagan

Our limitations are frequently only inside our head. Sometimes these limits—the things we believe we can't do—are more of a problem than our actual limitations. And it really doesn't matter where these limitations originated. They may be based on frustrations, poor teaching, biases from others, or just perceptions we felt about ourselves. The important thing is that we recognize they are there. We all have them.

As I've mentioned before when discussing personal limits, I am not talking about individuals who are aware of their potential but do not have any desire to move on in life. That is their choice. If someone chooses not to make progress to their goals—maybe they just want to watch TV or hang out—that is a choice. Deciding to not invest in yourself is self-selection; it's no one else's responsibility. You don't owe anybody anything, and nobody owes you anything for not participating.

And that's OK. As an economist, I would say that it is a person's right to choose whether they want to exert the effort to realize further potential. If they don't have sufficient information or understanding, perhaps books like this one will give them the insight to make decisions more aligned with their own best interests. These are people I want to help; it is a shame to see these people, particularly children, who unjustifiably don't believe in themselves.

Most people, in fact, probably have abilities far beyond what they are using and what they perceive is possible. As we grow, we set goals and expectations, but as we near realization of a goal, something happens. Your expectations are being met, so if you don't raise or adjust expectations, you will begin to plateau. That is, when you approach the expected level of your goal, you naturally tend to slow down and stop. In essence, you have arrived. Therefore, to continue making progress, you need to re-assess and adjust expectations to higher levels. Actually, as people are at or close to a goal, they often stay at that level for long periods of time. This is what's known as "plateauing."

Many people believe that being at a plateau, whether physical or mental, reflects the need for the body or mind to adjust to its new state. I do not believe that. I first encountered this phenomenon while I was a student at Berkeley, doing a great deal of weightlifting to reduce stress, which gave me considerably more energy for my studies. Whenever I found myself seemingly at a plateau in the amount of weight I was able to lift, I followed the advice of a former mentor and just raised the weight and the "plateau" was quickly pushed aside as I continued to make progress.

The real problem was that as I was reaching my goal or expectation, in my mind I thought that I was also reaching a plateau or limit for my body. But when I pushed aside the idea of a plateau and added more weight, I discovered that it clearly wasn't a plateau. I actually found it much easier to lift the heavier weight beyond the limit that my mind had convinced me was my plateau.

If you think you cannot get past something, your mind will actually accommodate you—and you will not pass it. The mind is like a huge computer that protects us. There are flight-or-fight responses when we are faced with threats. Similarly, there are also adjustments or rationalizations that the mind uses to protect us from potential disappointments or failures.

In track, for example, it was commonly thought for decades that running a mile in less than 4 minutes was beyond the limit of the human body. Then Roger Bannister cracked the 4-minute mark. At first, the world was stunned, but soon other runners realized it could be done. They moved up their pace slightly and broke the 4-minute barrier as well. Today, even a few high school athletes are able to run a sub-4 minute mile almost every year.

Limits are often thrust upon us by the expectations of others or by our own interpretations of events and beliefs. Sometimes, these expectations will set the tone that either restricts our progress—or it does the opposite, becoming a driving force to help us move forward. I overcame many physical and mental limits that I thought I had when growing up.

We face a dilemma. We may try to make decisions about our future, but simultaneously do not know what lies ahead, not having experienced it. Too many people will tell us to live in the moment and not to plan for the future. However, we cannot expect to make great decisions when we try to decide the future without thoroughly understanding both what is necessary to reach a goal, nor whether you will truly like or think it was worth it when you reach that goal. (This is one of the most important reasons to seek a mentor who can help guide you.)

In my own life, I've experienced two occasions where someone questioned me about spending in the present, versus saving and working for the future. The first time I was in the service and saving a lot of money. A fellow serviceman asked me, "Why are you saving? You could die tomorrow." My response was, "Yes, but what if I live?" Several years later, a second person asked the same question and my response was the same. I don't know how that first person turned out, but I can tell you about the second. He is now his

60s, living in abject poverty and not in very good health—the result of decades of trying to play the system to get free rides.

Nevertheless, the poor perceptions and prejudices of others often severely restrict our progress. We often think of bias in terms of restricting tangible opportunities, such as employment, access to funds, but the prejudice of others also leads to lower self-expectations. Just look around the country and see how different people are perceived. Southerners have an accent that some people in other areas of the country associate with lower intelligence.

Fortunately, some of that is changing. I believe the distribution of IQ's are the same everywhere, whether a ghetto or a remote small town. The difference is in expectations, environment and opportunity. Criticisms come in many ways and we need to wary of them. Watch when somebody criticizes a politician—not by arguing about their ideas, but by criticizing their speech patterns. Watch when someone criticizes another individual personally, rather than recognize a difference of opinion. People who do this are a cancer. If you have anyone like this in your life, start shrinking the time you spend with them. They will bring you down, even if their target is other people and not you.

If you are mired in a limiting belief of your own future, you really don't know how valid your self-perceptions are or how biased they are. One of my major goals is to get people to recognize the binds that are holding you down and to help you learn how to untie them. You may recall in the introduction to this book that I was very fortunate to run into a few people early on in my life who helped dispel me of my limits. But even with the encouragement I received, it still took great self-convincing and thought which made it seem possible to do well. I didn't know what "doing well" meant, nor what my potential was.

Remember, I felt that if I had less of a brain maybe rated a 90 versus what might be average, say 100, but work 20% harder than others, I could succeed. In essence, I would be at 10.8% effective brain capacity, whereas the average person would be at 10% of the average brain in terms of IQ. Whether this makes any sense biologically didn't matter, it gave me the motivation to hustle. Even then, it eventually took me almost 10 years to overcome the perceptions I had of myself. While I had several successes along the way, I continued to attribute those to very hard work, that idea of working 20% more than everyone else, rather than ability. That lasted for quite a long time.

Now I am not saying that everyone is going to go off and get a PhD at Berkeley, nor even have any desire to get one, but if you think you can't, you never will. What I am saying, is how limitations caused by poor perceptions severely restrict people's progress. Whatever your interest, you must "go for it." This is also where we develop self-confidence and belief in ourselves.

As mentioned in another example, think of all the people who feel they cannot learn a foreign language or who feel they can't learn it well—just as I once thought I couldn't.

Think of all the people who feel they are bad in math. I argue that almost every single person in high school today should be able to do well. For example, why is math so important? Part of it is the logic that will be embedded in your brain. Damn, I wish journalists and reporters had a lot more math and statistics. Then maybe I wouldn't see and hear so much stuff that makes no sense.

Well, how good do you really have to be? You should want to be very good, say an expert in what you are doing. But remember, you truly only need to be recognizably better than the next person. Actually, since most people recognize that the standards are much lower today; hard work can yield very significant success. To be truly among the top, set your own standards for how to be an expert. Don't let society or pre-determined systems set the standards, or you will limit your dreams. Break those limits and determine your own future.

When I was attending Hofstra University after military service, I was at my first final exam and a friend who had also returned from the military happened to be taking the same exam. When I admitted I was nervous he said, "Look around, this is our competition." Most of the students were gathered around before the exam in groups, joking and laughing about things. We were a little older; we knew the importance of what we were doing and were taking it more seriously. We were trying harder and working harder.

7

Developing the 'Why' in Your Life

What's your why? Why do you wake up in the morning? Why do you put on that jersey? Why do you go out and practice?
- Eric Thomas

What is your purpose in life—the "Why" that drives you to success?

As I've said previously, we are not talking about success as, say, being able to buy a new car or a new home. We are targeting success as a goal that is currently *outside* a person's immediate reach. When you create this goal, you may know where you would like to be, or what kind of life you would like to have—but you don't know the path to get there. Even before you know exactly where you are going, it's important to plan, even with contingencies.

One common example of such goals is America's effort to put a man on the moon. This is a great example of "breakthrough success." When this story is used as a motivational example, the emphasis is usually the thousands of course corrections that were needed to orbit and then land on the moon. That is not the significant part of that monumental goal. When President John F. Kennedy announced the ambitious dream, much of the technology needed to undertake this mission hadn't even been invented yet. There were huge, unknown holes in the knowledge we needed to accomplish this goal. We knew where we wanted to go, but had no idea yet how we were going to get there.

Later, when the trip to the moon was undertaken, we still had to make constant course corrections and adjustments to the plan. But ultimately, our drive for this success was not a breakthrough because of course corrections; it was through the decision to undertake a goal that was outside our nation's reach at the time. It was beyond where we could see a path to the end goal. True breakthrough success will take monumental efforts and will be a series of smaller goals. It's not a foregone conclusion, then, that everyone is willing to put in the effort to attain that new or different life. If someone truly is changing their life and that may mean environment too, it will take that tremendous effort.

So what is this "Why" we are talking about? First, it's all about defining your dreams, what you really want, without considering any restrictions. Ask yourself where your current dreams or goals were originally born. Has my goal been drawn by my parents, my friends or spouse, or is it truly mine? To reach a goal that is truly out of sight, it must be completely your own. It is only if it is within you, that you will be able to break through any barriers.

There are many actions you can take to achieve your dreams. Just make sure you're not coerced or unduly influenced to do a specific thing you really don't want, because then what you're doing will waste your time, effort, and energy on things that are unnecessary and create a result you may never like. Your heart won't be in it. And the likelihood of achieving it will be greatly reduced if it truly doesn't come from inside you. Conversely, don't judge anybody else's goals; hopefully, it is what they truly desire based on their values.

The "Why" is the very existence or purpose in our life—the reason behind and the driving force in everything a person does to move them ahead or towards a goal. By this we mean a purpose that is beyond our ability to see how to get to that goal. Is it truly a dream—like putting a man on the moon—or is it something you already feel or know you can do?

A dream can be defined in terms of a combination of family, financial, location, reputation and many other things. It's not only what you want to be, but a picture of what your dream looks like when you reach it. What does your job, home, family and life in general, look like? If this reminds you of childhood dreaming, you're on the right track. You're dreaming about your future life, and you have no idea how to get there yet; you may need to invent things or create tools and skills that don't exist and achieve things that you don't realize yet are in your path. Don't worry. In a later chapter, we'll focus on setting goals, and building a pathway of smaller steps to accomplish your dream—not just achievement but breakthrough success.

Recognize, too, that your dream may change over time. It probably will. My own dream changed significantly, but that didn't matter to my successes. Changes will inevitably result from the experiences you have while moving toward any goal.

Most people set goals for their future in high school or college—without even understanding what the goal really is. They see some television shows with lawyers in court rooms or negotiating some big deals. They think they want to practice law, but don't see the massive amounts of research and writing that must be done. Is that something they do or would enjoy? Or they see nurses depicted as young women tirelessly caring for patients, while they somehow manage to keep their makeup intact. Or scientists pictured as making some amazing discovery, without trying and failing for years, or being under someone else's scrutiny and lacking independence. This images are not exactly realistic.

I am not saying these aren't great goals. They may be for someone, not for someone else. The point is, we actually develop our dreams and goals over time as we learn and grow. Early life goals are the dreams that are made without even truly understanding what they are. Is it any wonder that we change?

As we go through the years, into our late teens or early 20s, we still don't understand thoroughly where we are going or understand what will be there when we reach our goal. Think of all the college students majoring in fields that lead nowhere. They had no realistic idea of where they were going or what life would be like when they arrived. Unfortunately, many of them were aided and supported in their decision by their parents.

We need to go back to pretending to be a child, once again dreaming about what life we would truly like. I don't mean conjuring a castle on the hill nor do I mean focusing on the money that makes it obtainable. Of course, earning sufficient income to live well can be a reasonable goal for a time. Throughout your life, you keep revising your goals. If you are moving forward and growing, this makes your life broader and richer by opening up more avenues from which you may choose what purpose fulfills you.

Now if you're reading this chapter and you are not in your late teens or early 20s, but rather 40, this still relates to you. Your current situation is a product of what you have done over the last 10-plus years. Consider this: Would you like to be in the same situation in 10 years that you are today? Keep in mind, with life spans today reaching past 90 years of age, you have 50-plus years to go. Most goals can be accomplished if they are thought of as 10-year goals, but when you are older a 10-year goal can be scary because you don't know how to get there—and your lifespan is shorter. Still, you can develop smaller five-year and near-term goals to build the path. I'm not saying you can do *anything*. If you are 40, it is too late to plan a professional basketball or football career. There are other things that will be out of reach too. But don't focus on that.

When dreaming of that 10-year goal or lifetime goal, you need to ask yourself some questions. Will you be happy? If your purpose is only based on material things, it will not be as strong as one based on how you feel when that goal is accomplished.

Your long-term goal should be formulated as if time and money were not an impediment and it was not possible to fail. Granted, you will probably see some immediate and significant problems that might interfere with your ability to complete your goal. But as you recall in the previous chapter, most weaknesses can be sufficiently fixed. Right now you have no idea where your goal may take you, since you'll be learning new things and envisioning even more opportunities on the path to that goal; ultimately, these experiences may change your directions.

Despite such experiences, I have seen many people who decide not to attempt to change their lifestyle or expand their opportunities. It is not for us to judge their choices—nor is it right for them to judge or complain about those who want to make these lifestyle changes. Perhaps you, too, are reluctant to develop the lifetime goal I'm asking of you because it is beyond your current understanding of how to accomplish it. I agree, that is scary. But think of the process like chapters of this book: They're based on many facets of my life, not only the learning and experiences, but the outstanding knowledge from successful people in varied fields. If you take this book seriously and use it, you will have experiences of mine and others and build out your own book, and your life as you expand beyond me.

At this point, let's talk in more detail about how to solidify your "Why."
Generally, people need to make their goals visual. You want something concrete, something you can look at that reminds you what you are targeting. One highly recommended method is to create a "vision board" that illustrates what you want in your life. This board is a collection of your personal dreams, again with no restrictions—literally, pictures and phrases of your future that are displayed on a board and kept in a place you will see every day.

Your vision board combines many facets for your life, including finances, family, health, home and career. Cut out the images and quotes that remind you of these goals from magazines or download them from the Internet. Now go beyond the vision board and bring reality to your dreams. If your goals include a better car or house, go to open houses and new-car dealerships as a motivator. Make your dreams real.

Yes, your dreams will change, but because you are learning more and making progress along the way.

As an example, let me share with you how some of my dreams for a home changed. Like many people, I dreamed of owning a somewhat secluded home in the country. Over time, as I learned more about myself, I considered potential hazards such as forest fires and how I would feel if not just my home, but its contents, were destroyed. Also, I realized that if I had secluded home, the time it would take to drive to activities that I might continue to enjoy later in life would be too much. Since I really love cooking, I would need to be near places with good supplies at good prices and professional quality. That might seem silly or irrelevant to someone else, but that's called personal choice.

Additionally, I still love the idea of having a large home. Yet the idea of having such a home where I might need people living in it or having frequent access for maintenance, for cleaning or care would be much more of an impingement on my privacy than I would prefer. So while moving toward my dreams of a huge home, I learned that I wanted something different. Not only was I *not* jealous nor disappointed in not reaching those initial goals; I was actually happier because I understood my own preferences better. (By the way, I do have that great kitchen I wanted and have great supplies within 10 minutes from multiple sources and with 3,500 square feet instead of some huge home.)

Your life goals, too, probably will change over time. That's okay. What's important that you are driving towards a goal. Like everyone else, you will have earth-shattering setbacks and disappointments. Breaking through these will require more than just your vision board and some tours of new homes. In the next chapter, we look at how to take your fears and make them a positive motivator.

8
How to Make Failure Not an Option!

'Failure is not an option'

~ attributed to Gene Kranz, but actually from the movie, Apollo 13

Most books about motivation will tell you to focus on your goal, but for many reasons, this approach usually fails. Think about all the people who try to lose weight, stop drinking, stop smoking, exercise more, or the myriad other changes people want to make in life. Think about all the failed New Year's resolutions people. The same people make the same resolution every year, and over 90% of them fail within three weeks. And your chance of success would be bleak, too, if you were just focused on another short-term goal.

Most people don't succeed based on just having dreams. People really need something much stronger and a reason that their current situation or their apparent future seems unacceptable. Actually, it must be much stronger than just "unacceptable," because the degree of distaste for their current situation will correlate with their drive to move forward. While this chapter may seem negative, it also may be one of the most important, because it builds on the motivation that drives most people.

First, let's look more closely at the type of goals people make for their New Year's resolutions. They are usually the number-one priority for a person at the time. Also, they are relatively simple in comparison to the kind of life-changing goals we are discussing in this book. Yet, these itsy-bitsy, minor-league goals don't even last three weeks! So clearly, we need to do something quite different if we're really targeting big goals.

Why do many people fail at such attempts?

Well, some of them spend their time complaining—no matter the situation or challenge—about whatever life presents them. Whether you are in the group that always complains or finds excuses for failure, or in the group that really feels they are trying to succeed, 90% don't even make it. Everyone needs a strong reason and a good mirror to see themselves and take responsibility for their situation.

There is another reason, however, that explains why few people achieve their goals, let alone achieve the heights that are beyond their current vision. They are not driven by a dream and they don't have sufficient drive to leave their current situation. And especially when they are young, most people are unprepared to take action on their own. Something had to drive them to success, even a weak success.

Think of the areas where most people succeed. Those successes tend to include well-defined projects and goals, whether at school or at work. While you were in school, what was your process for getting things done—that is, succeeding? When did you study for an exam? When did you finish a research report? Did you get your schoolwork done just in time before the due date? How many people actually finished it early in order to refine the work and make it exemplary?

Why did the 'A' students get their work done early and refine it? Is it because they were 'A' students? Or did they become 'A' students *because* they did it early and refined it? This book is dedicated to showing that most people can be an 'A' student—or successful in almost every arena—with the right tools.

At home, most chores and tasks are defined by parents, who usually bestow a reward or punishment in response to their completion. Did you or your parents decide whether you would be allowed to go out once your chores were done or your room was clean? Overall, most of the goals you had during your early life probably had their terms set by others. But as adults, we must be the ones to choose the motivators that drive ourselves toward a desired outcome.

This is not an easy transition. In fact, when we leave school or home, we enter one of the most difficult periods of life. Most deadlines and goals become much less clear and less frequent. Independence means that for the first time, we must determine our own goals, starting in areas such as career and family. No longer is there somebody that maps out our path. Now, we need to develop not only our own set of goals, but our consequences for *not* meeting those goals. That's right—we must understand or envision the outcome if we do *not* meet our goals.

It's easy to see how adjusting our goals can easily lead us to lower expectations. People do it all the time. In school, we may start a semester imagining that we will get our A or B+, but we adjust our goals downward and fill our minds with reasons why they weren't possible.

The human brain has a fascinating way of adapting. The brain adjusts to disappointments and helps us redefine expectations so that we can maintain our sanity—or at least feel more comfortable. That is what we discussed in the chapter on limits. Also, we sometimes find ourselves rationalizing what happens to us, so the unacceptable becomes acceptable; we make excuses for ourselves. Unfortunately, the brain is so good at helping us adjust our expectations that we can quickly end up with lesser goals, cheating ourselves of the future we truly desire and could attain.

Our friends or acquaintances can help us cope with failure or disappointment, and while this soothing may feel good, it doesn't help us move forward and succeed. Look at your Facebook timeline on any given day. Some friend is talking about a difficulty they're facing, and everyone tries to cheerlead. If a person gets fired, all their friends tell them their boss was terrible and it was an awful place—even though their friends know almost nothing about their work. I've had a number of people tell me about their friend's terrible workplace and I usually ask, "Were you there? Have you been to their workplace?" The answer always is, "No, they told me." So, how do you know what happens? You don't, and you are not helping a friend by agreeing with their downward spiral. Maybe it was a bad place; listening and encouraging is good. Enabling is not good. With all of this, it is clear you need to develop something that gives motivation to move forward in the right direction.

    We need to develop a more effective means of motivation for confronting the prospect of *not* meeting our goals: fear. Fear can actually be one of the most effective motivators toward achieving success. Do we get up and go to work every day because we love it? What kind of motivations do we actually have? We are usually afraid of the consequences of not showing up to work, or of not being successful—and how that will appear to our friends and family.

Many people are motivated by the fear of sheer survival or by the fear of not attaining what they feel they need. Before rampant grade inflation, it was the fear of summer school or being left back a grade that made students study hard. Today, teachers often don't want students to be upset by their performance on exams and in the classroom. So, students generally experience neither the stress of complete failure nor the consequences of it. Would you really expect outstanding results from that kind of system?

A word of caution here: There is a delicate balance between being motivated by the fear and being immobilized by it. We don't want to elicit motivation entirely by fear; relying on it too much could be devastating. But, we may need to depend on it heavily as a start and to get through some of the most difficult times. When I was going to language school in the military, the fear, based on threat, was that if anyone failed they would be sent to infantry training and off to a war zone. Since most of our motivators in the past were based on the fear of certain consequences, it is perfectly normal to build a set of fears to go along with our goals in order to greatly enhance the probability of our reaching those goals.

Basic fears should be used as a motivator to help you make better decisions about life, to prevent you from quitting or deserting your goals. What you're actually doing is using fear as a means of keeping you on schedule and maintaining your progress. At some point, you will build up a sufficient number of successes and enough confidence to keep the fear of failure from even entering your mind. It is then called "confidence." Eventually, you will attain that attitude that you can do anything or nearly anything and will figure a way to accomplish new goals outside your comfort zone. In the meantime, you need to push yourself with some fear, so you don't end up missing a goal.

Still, fear is a complex issue, and it's important to note that it can infringe on your creativity as well as your productivity. You don't want to suffer the bad effects of fear, so how do you avoid this? You need to transform the negativity of fear into a positive source of motivation; you must make fear part of the framework of your goals. Keep in the back of your mind, and maybe even on an index card, a reminder.

Consider, for example, the difference between fearfully cramming for an exam and using fear to *avoid* the cramming experience. You can use fear to avoid cramming by reminding yourself that if you don't do X, Y, and Z, you will have to cram at the end of the year. But that will probably not be enough. You will need to create daily and weekly goals that are clearly defined so that at the end of the course your overall goal is truly met.

Right before I started college, I took advice from a book on how to study for exams. I learned that it was important not to cram, and that the night before an exam, it was important to relax. From that time, I never studied after 6 p.m. the night before an exam. There was really nothing to learn. This was a simple recipe created by someone who knew. So I copied the recommendations and just followed them. How could this be possible to not need to study the night before an exam? As the book explained, throughout a course you should prepare for each class, get questions answered during the class, and review your notes within two hours of the end of the class. If you did that, retention of material was approximately 80 percent. If you waited until the next day to review the material, your retention was approximately 20 percent.

Since material for a course is normally taught sequentially and is a prerequisite for forthcoming material, let's look at what would happen if you did not review the material shortly after each class. Throughout the semester, as you go from one class to the next, the course material usually becomes more difficult—and you're retaining only 20% of the material each time. Furthermore, the increasing difficulty of new material is compounded, because it's usually dependent on much of what you learned before but forgot.

When exams approach, you are in a state of near panic (or should be) and the only solution appears to be cramming. Simultaneously, you need to cram for other exams, too. You are in a state of panic. You must now set goals, spurred by the fear of doing badly on the exams and the consequences. So you resort to cramming—perhaps hoping for the good luck of correctly guessing what questions the professor will choose!

This is not a path to success. You're not looking at how well you understand the subject matter but merely how to pass the exam. Instead, consider what would happen if you were the student who prepares ahead, asks questions and reviews within two hours of the class. You would retain most of the material. And since you would have a better understanding of the material, you would then find it easier and less time-consuming to study new material. With this type of preparation, your questions would be for clarification rather than survival. Over time, you'd be filling in the holes in your knowledge, rather than trying to relearn prerequisite material in order to understand something new. Imagine how this could build over a semester, the confidence you would gain. In the end you're the one pulling the course together to understand the subject matter, while the student who crammed is in a state of near-panic, asking his friends, "What do you think will be on the test?"

If you crammed all the way through college like many people, that means you were driven only by deadlines and consequences imposed by outside forces. You will need to learn to develop your own motivators. What's going to drive you in the real world? You must learn to set your own goals and your own time constraints. As you grow up, you need to be able to set your own terms for evaluating what is truly possible, because learning in life is a never-ending process. It is important to enjoy the success of meeting each step, patting yourself on the back along the way. After all, happiness is the realization of successfully achieved outcomes; it is the achievement of your goals in life, one at a time.

Large goals can be extremely difficult, since there is too much time between the starting point and the point where you finally achieve success. To attain larger, long-term goals, these goals must be broken down into targeted steps, which must be broken down further into sufficiently smaller steps so that the completion of each builds and reinforces confidence through a series of successes.

Consider what I've done with this book. After creating my outline, I drafted a schedule for the completion of each chapter. Then, for each chapter, I created a schedule for note-taking, outlining, drafting, and rewriting. My goal was to finish the book. But if I looked only at the end goal, I am certain that the difficulty of writing would have overwhelmed me. But by dividing the process of writing into steps I knew that I could achieve, I was able to continually see realistic progress toward a successful outcome. Yes, life often got in the way of writing this book, but by having smaller goals, the path to interrupted completion was always a reality.

As we work toward our goals, there are a number of fears we can use to motivate ourselves. Take poverty, for example. One of the things I did while going to college was drive through poorer neighborhoods just to remind myself on a regular basis that this is *not* what I wanted for my future. As I looked at the homes in the neighborhood, I would think about the lives of the people who lived there and what life would be like in these neighborhoods. What were their daily and weekly lives like? What were their vacations like? I knew many of them. They probably had no more than two weeks' vacation per year and frequently stayed home or visited family or friends nearby. Their weekends were probably not filled with taking spur-of-the-moment trips to places like Hawaii,

San Diego or skiing. They may have gone swimming locally at a public pool or to the beach, or they may have had backyard barbecues. They may have gone camping, but they wouldn't have gone to Hawaii or the Caribbean. If they did, it would have been a once-in-a-lifetime situation.

The people in these homes probably had significantly low lifestyle ceilings—and I'm not referring to the ceilings of their home, but the ceilings on the lives themselves. You have heard of the "glass ceiling" that women experience in their careers. Well, for these people there are concrete ceilings that will not be broken through. Most of these people worked in local plants, factories, or stores. Even if their level of responsibility at work increased, they were not going to get paid much more than the average salary.

I would say to myself that these were places where most people had not completed college with strong grades or perhaps never had the opportunity to go to college. How true this was, I don't know. But this fear was an important source of motivation for me: It was a reminder of what would happen to me if I didn't succeed.

When I started graduate school for my Ph.D. at U.C. Berkeley, I quickly recognized that all the other students were graduated from Harvard, MIT, Cornell, Princeton, Stanford and Berkeley. They already completed or audited the first-year graduate courses. These graduate-level courses were not even available at Hofstra University where I went. It didn't have a graduate program. I didn't even know what the courses would contain. I again used the same technique for motivation that I used at Hofstra. This time the fear was if I didn't make it, I would be back in the same situation with that neighborhood lifestyle. I didn't communicate my fears to my family. While I did not want to disappoint them, as I think back, they would have acted like friends on Facebook. Meaning well and not wanting me to feel badly, they would have made quitting or failure a legitimate option. I reminded myself that failure was not an option. There were times during that first year that I was extremely stressed wondering if I would survive.

Ultimately, while wonderful images of the future and great expectations can help you progress toward your goals, there are inevitably going to be some difficult times. To achieve breakthrough success, you must venture into unknown areas and encounter unexpected obstacles along the way. To endure some of these extraordinary times and surpass these challenges, you'll probably find yourself saying to yourself at times: "Failure is not an option. I must succeed." This often is the driving force behind the early path to success for many true champions.

9

Wisdom Versus Knowledge

'Wisdom is not a product of schooling but of the lifelong attempt to acquire it.'
~ Albert Einstein

One day when I was about 13, I was sitting in church, wondering why people had to continually relearn lessons of the past. I recall that the sermon dealt with some great wisdom of the past. It made me curious as to why there were some mistakes that would be made over and over again, generation after generation. I sat there thinking: How can we learn from the past?

Wouldn't it be nice if everything that was done by our parents, teachers or mentors could be explained to us or written down so we wouldn't have to learn through the same mistakes they made? Think about this: For centuries people have made the same mistakes that people before them made. Why can't we just see those mistakes and not repeat them? Why do we not follow the advice of those with experience?

Because these mistakes cannot be learned, except through experiences that grow into wisdom.

I recognize that this chapter may sound somewhat like a philosophical lesson, but it will give you an important foundation to accelerate your progress toward success. For our purposes, I am defining wisdom here as that which you understand, but cannot be deduced, explained or proven through logical discourse. On the other hand, knowledge is something that you can understand through reading a book or listening to verbal discourse. This is my definition; I am not willing to debate it. I did look up many definitions and discourses on knowledge and wisdom. While it seems that they can fit under this definition as well, most of the definitions or distinctions that I read were more useful only for philosophical debate. That is not my goal here; I want to uphold wisdom as a means to success. What is the difference between how we acquire wisdom and knowledge and how can we use it to accelerate our progress?

It would be wonderful if experiences and understanding over years could be passed from one generation to the next. Can you imagine where society and technology would be if our energy and time weren't wasted on many of life's re-learned lessons? Think of the progress you would have made, if all the tasks you needed to learn in life could be drawn from the experiences of your parents, and you were able to do them correctly—the first time. Unfortunately, your parents or mentors were not able to convince you of the right path, nor will you be able to explain it to your children. There appear to be some things that just can't be logically or unequivocally explained.

    I've spent much time thinking about this topic and it's greatly affected my education and my philosophy about learning. I've come to realize the importance of finding and choosing mentors—people you can learn from or copy from in order to accelerate your own progress. And I've realized the importance of respecting their opinions and recommendations, in spite of not always understanding the logic behind them.

    Let's say, for example, that you're sitting with a teacher or senior colleague you respect. You feel you should take a certain path in approaching a problem, whether it's the way to present an argument or a research paper. This mentor, however, has much more experience and recommends a different direction. Even with lengthy discussion, neither of you can prove to the other which approach is right; neither of you can logically prove your idea. Most people will choose their own path over that of the more experienced person. But is that really the best choice?

If this person is substantially more experienced and you truly respect their background, it may be a more logical choice to choose their recommendation over your own, even if you can't explain it. This is what I realized about wisdom sitting in church that day, and it has benefited me many times over.

I had just such an experience while involved in politics as a student at Hofstra University. Occasionally, I would have conversations with a political science professor, Dr. Herbert Rosenbaum, sometimes for political advice, other times just to test ideas. Once, when I was the faculty representative to the board of trustees, the university was involved in deciding a fairly major financial issue. (Yes, although I was a student, I was elected as one of the two faculty representatives to the board of trustees.) I had a lengthy and thorough debate with Dr. Rosenbaum about this topic, and in the end, he could not prove his recommendation was better than mine, nor could I prove mine was superior. As chairman of the University Budget and Planning Committee, I was tasked with bringing a recommendation to committee—as with many things, it was something that you only have one shot to get right. After leaving his office that day, I decided to take his path rather than my own. Why? I had the utmost respect for him, not only because of his knowledge, but also because of his wisdom.

The following week when I saw him again, he asked me what I had decided to do. He was quite surprised that I took his idea, rather than my own, because we had argued quite a bit. I explained that whichever path I chose I would still learn. However, since I could not logically prove that mine was better, wouldn't it be better to take the one chosen by somebody I truly respected, a person who had a great deal more experience and wisdom? Remember, this was one of those situations in life where you did not get a "do- over." When you were a little kid and the outcome of a game wasn't what you desired or expected, it was often acceptable to call for a do-over and try again. As adults, life is not that easy. In any public setting, especially, you can't redo something or take back your words, and even if you could redo something, it will often have an adverse impact or leave a poor impression.

If you do get a chance to try something over again, you are still wasting the most precious resource you have—time. Once your time is spent, it can never be reclaimed. Isn't that that the essence of this chapter? If we can avoid it, we shouldn't waste our time trying to relearn the lessons that historically were learned by others. In circumstances where we greatly respect the success and experience, we should rely on their wisdom.

It's important not only to distinguish the differences between knowledge and wisdom, but to be careful not to fall in love with your own ideas, unless you can truly prove them to others. Imagine that you could step aside from yourself and think of a debate in terms of a bet. Who should you really bet will have the correct or better answer: yourself or the person you chose to mentor you? In my own case, since wisdom is based on experience and I clearly was at a disadvantage, what person in their right mind would bet on my strategy versus my Hofstra mentor's?

If you use that notion as part of your decision-making process, you may find yourself changing some of your decisions by taking advantage of the wisdom of others. In the end, if you can remove your ego and bring yourself to use this concept, you can truly accelerate your own progress. The reason most people seek out mentors or advisors is to learn how to do something successfully. Given that reasoning, it might be foolish *not* to take their advice, if you cannot conclusively prove your own case.

Part II

TAKING ACTION

10

Set Your Goals by Reaching for the Stars

'If you aim for Number 1, you might make only 3 or 4, but if you aim for the top ten, you'll probably never get there'
~ Thomas O'Grady, PhD

In Part 1 of this book, I emphasized the importance of reaching for the stars when you set goals in life—that is, you need to decide what you truly want and set your sights at the top without any qualification. Now, I want to talk to you more in depth about the specific action steps needed to achieve your goals.

Goal-setting generally comes in three stages. Stage 1 can be described as setting out a target but having no idea if you can or how to attain it. Remember, this a true goal for "Breakthrough Success," not the typical goal where you can see how to achieve it. Stage 2 is where you identify what you need to know, what skills you have and don't have yet, to achieve your goal. Along the path to success, you will almost certainly require some more things or skills you need that you don't even know yet. And, Stage 3 is where you can actually visualize yourself at the goal, crossing the finish line. You see yourself with the rewards, accolades and self-satisfaction of being there. After you just finished the self-assessment stages, where do you currently see yourself having achieved your end goal or dream? You need to picture the finish line even if you don't know yet how you will get there. It is important to understand that it is necessary to reach Stage 3, or you will never realize the type of goal to which I among referring.

As I pointed out in Chapter 6, (Developing Your Why) most people limit themselves by setting goals based on what they already know they can attain, or that which they feel is potentially attainable. There may be some goals, such as becoming superbly fit, that you'll never reach, but you can still figure out all the pieces you need to reach them. I am not referring to these goals. In Stage 1, I'm challenging you to reach for the top, to imagine and dream beyond the expectations you currently have of yourself. Go for the gold. Quit going after what you already know. Instead, you will want to figure out how to get to where you *really* would like to be. At this time, make that goal a real stretch; you don't have to know how to get there. The path and skills you need can be figured out later.

If the goal is to be an architect, consider not only what it takes to be a master builder, designing a major bridge, the Willis Tower or Disney World. If your goal is to be an electrician or plumber, aim to be a master electrician or master plumber. If your goal is to be a musician, your goal should be to be among the elite, not just among those who are considered good.

Why aim for the very top, rather than a "reasonable" goal?

Because if you aim to be in the top 10, you'll probably never make the top 5. Aim to be No. 1, whatever your goal, and if you do miss, you might be No. 2 or No. 3. But you will also have a greater and more enjoyable journey. You'll have a better understanding of what it means to be among the best. Otherwise, you might find yourself talking about what "could have been" or thinking about what you "could have done."

Next, the job in Stage 2 is to figure out how to get there. What does it take to be the best? Whether you're younger or well into your working years, if your goal is to be a lawyer or doctor, for example, what is the best path to becoming the best? Are you after a degree in order to say you are one of these professionals, or do you desire the pride that radiates confidence when you see others in the same field admire your accomplishments? The more successful you are as you move along, whether it was back in college or later in a career, the more opportunities will open for you. Yes, that means you need to strive for the best in all relevant work and study you do.

Continuing with the college example, you need to consider what law school or medical school would be best for you? You should aim for the best school that is consistent with being the best as the kind of professional you would like to be. What undergraduate school would be best to prepare you and get you into one of those schools? And once you're at that undergraduate school, what grades and other skills do you need to qualify yourself for the graduate program you want?

There are many undergraduate schools that will never get you into a top professional or graduate school. Conversely, there are schools with great records for placement into prestigious graduate programs.

For example, when I served as a member of the Hofstra University Board of Trustees and Chairman of the Budget and Planning Committee, I had access to data about the college's success getting students admitted to medical schools. At the time, it was extremely difficult to get admitted to medical school, but I learned that Hofstra had an extremely high success rate and therefore was a great entry point for students who wanted to become doctors. (Unfortunately for Hofstra, they didn't use any of that great information effectively as I thought they could in their marketing materials.)

From the very beginning of school, learning new skills or improving existing ones is necessary, because in three years you will have an exam, and at that time you won't be able to study for those skills. For aspiring lawyers, the test is the LSAT; for students applying to graduate school, it's the GRE; and for students entering medical or dental school, there are other exams. You must develop skills and fill yourself with the necessary knowledge to shine. What skills will you need, in addition to writing, speaking, and logic? Think back to the points I emphasized in the earlier chapter, "Know Your Weaknesses and Go on a Diet." Now, combining the skills needed and the grades needed, you may have to learn some skills before you go to college or continue the education process during the summers. You may not be able to afford a poor grade in something that you struggle through. That must be considered. It could kill your average and your chances of getting into a graduate program of your choice.

Once you're out of school and taking steps toward your goal—whether it's a position working in a corporation or another firm or starting your own business—you will still be looking to discover the skills needed and to find the mentors who can help you develop those skills. First, re-examine your goal and the path you need to reach it. What is the top? What can the people at the top do? What do they know, have access to, and use as tools? Armed with this material, you now need to determine how others reached the pinnacle of success in the area that contains your goal. The best ways to accomplish this are to read about people who have done it and to find some of them. When you feel you have some intelligent questions, ask them. Or go on social media, like Twitter, follow people whom you respect and whose goals reflect your aspirations. How do you get to know these people? Ask questions, look for opportunities to meet them at professional or social events—one encounter often leads to another.

One of your goals at this time should be to find a mentor, regardless of your position in life. To do this, you don't just ask someone if you can be their mentee. After some preparation, ask them some reasonably intelligent questions, and you might be on a path to gaining a mentor. Be straightforward, and ask, "If I have another question sometime in the future, may I contact you?" If you have looked over and written down the skills and experiences you need for a certain position, you will have some good questions. If you are looking for a position in a trade, you might find that instructor and ask your question. If so, you just made a contact.

As I've discussed earlier, it is important not to be bogged down by unfounded beliefs about what you *cannot* do, unless you are truly constrained by a handicap. It is also important not to be bogged down with other people's excuses or reasons for why you can't achieve your goals. Let's revisit the story of my Russian friend, Leon, that I first mentioned in Chapter 4. Leon came up to me one day to ask a very telling question about Americans: "Why do Americans brag about being bad at math?" He reiterated, "I mean, they don't just say it. They are *proud* to be saying they are bad at math." What was I to say? Well, if you know me, I did what you would expect. I replied, "They are stupid"—not for being bad at math, but rather for not being a little embarrassed to say they cannot or didn't try to do well. The level of math needed to get through high school is attainable by anyone. The only reason people don't do well is because they either don't know how to learn the skills, weren't taught well, or didn't care.

An individual's performance in math is a strong example of how expectations can affect one's ability in a wide variety of areas, including languages. Remember, I was terrible at language in high school, but was taught the skills needed to learn a language at the Defense Language Institute in Monterey. That was awesome. And, I saw the same change in skill level with several high school students who felt they were not good at math.

What I want to emphasize here is that most people exclude themselves from most opportunities. You may never be a mathematician, a United Nations translator or a professional writer, but don't exclude anything when you may only need to do reasonably well in an area of a current weakness. Envision the final goal. First, decide what you need to do to get to where you want to be. Before anybody puts any limitations on your own expectations, you want to know what it takes to be the best. You mustn't short-change yourself and your future. The puzzle of how to achieve your dream can be solved by breaking down your path into several steps and determining what is needed at each stage. You will determine what additional skills are needed as you progress down your path, and hopefully, you will already be working on them if you previously identified any of them as a weakness.

Part of this process is to help you figure out whether you will be happy with your original goal and if you want to continue the work needed to reach it. For example, there is a tremendous amount of writing and research involved in becoming a lawyer. Do you even want to do that? As you work toward your goal, you will probably reset it, placing it higher or in a slightly different direction as you learn. There were times I reset my goals and therefore the skills I was learning. The process of really modifying or resetting my goals is the result of learning, developing skills and understanding new targets. I can still benefit from prior skills learned and the process of learning itself.

Now let me re-emphasize what I've said earlier: I am using "goals" here as an end point. But while you have an overall goal of where you want to finally arrive, there will also be many intermediate goals. All your goals, big and small, short- and long-term, are synonymous with steps of success. While I am referring primarily to career goals, they could be physical or financial goals, or related to relationship and family, or they could be based on self-development. And while you aim for the top in whatever you choose, it may change as you learn about yourself and that's all right. My goals changed at times, but the skills I learned in the past continued to help me.

Goals are simply targets to improve your life and surroundings. A homemaker (either husband or wife), for example, may aim to take care of the household, manage the finances, and raise the children. A goal for raising children could be to help them become the best they can be with a great positive attitude and real-world survival skills. The goals of a mother (or father) include providing a strong education for the children and maintaining their health, as well as attending to the myriad responsibilities of the household. Simultaneously, if the parent has a spouse, she or he must maintain this partnership through shared interests.

When you set goals, you are preparing to undertake actions that will have a positive effect on your life, your family and friends. You are attempting to enhance the present by creating something that you can look forward to accomplishing. While you must acknowledge your limitations, don't automatically accept them as a final sentence. You must constantly draw inspiration from imagining the completed goal, how it feels, and what it yields when you have achieved it. For inspiration, keep an eye out for all the success stories of people overcoming limitations. Are the limitations true or real or can they be overcome? You can take comfort as you can find others who have overcome them. This is Stage 3, where you can actually see yourself at the goal, crossing the finish line. There are countless stories of people who overcame adversity or even negative expectations. Let your goals be your own driving force and seek out the people who can help and ignore the naysayers.

You want to be around only the people that see a glass as half full. Michael Jordan was told by his high school's basketball coach that he should do something else as he would never be a basketball player. He became the greatest basketball player of all time. Nick Vijicic is a man born without limbs and became an inspiration for others. (If you think you have limitations, look him up!) Jennifer Bricker was born without legs and became a state champion gymnast. Think of all the people who come to this country and don't know the language and usually don't have any support network—and in spite of these limitations, they succeed.

To attain your goal you will need to develop fortitude, decisiveness, and perseverance. You need mental and emotional strength to succeed, even to make the decision to reach the goal, barring any obstacles. But that strength alone is not enough; you also need the perseverance and determination to see your journey through. That is, you realize and understand there will be blockages, setbacks, and unexpected obstacles. This is when your fears, your "why not" from the earlier chapter, become so important as a motivator that they will keep you from sliding backward or giving up; that is, your personal reason for why "failure truly is not an option."

Finally, take notice of the patience, determination, and persistence that your young child—even your dog—may demonstrate. Are you going to show that you are smarter than they are? Your children learned to walk because they constantly were encouraged. You may need to find that same encouragement from others, which may mean new "friends" or other sources.

Always remember, you can learn something from everyone. In a later chapter, we will talk much more about surrounding yourself with supportive and knowledgeable people and making new friends to help you on your journey. But, for this chapter, before you go another step, make a preliminary decision on your long-term dream. Whatever you are today was predominantly determined by your last 10 years. Whatever you want to become should be able to be completed in the next 10 years.

11

Step Out of Your 'Comfort Zone'

'Your perspective on life comes from the cage you were held captive in'
~ Shannon L. Alder

Psychologists often refer to a person's "comfort zone," but what does that really mean?

It's not just the definition that is important, but how it makes you feel, how it limits your growth, controls your relationships and how other's comfort zones control you. By definition, our comfort zone is where we feel the best and where we are usually found to reside. That is, it's what is familiar to us.

Our individual comfort zone is shaped by our past experiences, our friendships, our families and our environment. Shaped by our friends and family, our comfort zone is largely similar to the zones of those people. After all, we are moving in the same circles, doing the same things and generally avoiding the same things. Logically, we live together with others largely within this comfort zone; otherwise we would not feel good while engaging in any activities with them.

But while the comfort zone makes us feel safe, it also limits our growth and, in effect, our progress in life. The common expression, "stepping outside the box," implies that somebody is trying something new—and that it will be uncomfortable. Yet education requires us to go through an uncomfortable phase. Continuous education means you are continuously uncomfortable. And in striving for continuous improvement, we are intentionally, continuously, uncomfortable. So you can see that the desire to grow actually requires us to *love* being uncomfortable.

It does sound strange to say that people would intentionally make themselves uncomfortable. When we hear it, it almost seems to be masochistic, like some type of psychological disorder. Is this analogous to hurting ourselves? Well, of course not, but it certainly sounds strange. To understand this apparent paradox, let's look more closely at how a comfort zone works.

Picture a person who is comfortable. There are things they will do, and other things they may or may not do that make them uncomfortable. Picture the comfort zone as a person represented by a dot with a circle around this dot. Yes, there really are many more dimension one might consider or that may affect them, but this is a good representation. The larger the circle, the larger that person's comfort zone. Anything within the circle is within the person's comfort zone. The circle itself represents the limit. If we attempt to push out at any point on the circle, we are going into new territory and creating an uncomfortable situation— that is, a new experience.

When the person understands the new area, they are learning. Think about the very idea of learning: while helping us to understand the unknown, education, by definition, is uncomfortable until we complete the learning process. Change, in general, makes people uncomfortable. Some welcome it, others do not. But if we recede into our comfort zone, we limit ourselves and don't grow. To grow in any area or field, we need to embrace going outside the comfort zone—and this lesson should begin in childhood. We must raise our children so they see the process of breaking out of their comfort zone as challenging as exciting; the goal of learning is to embrace being uncomfortable.

Actually, the desire to stay within our comfort zone is one of the most deterring effects for progress or growth in many parts of our society. For example, every large company develops some sort of culture. By definition, that culture creates a comfort zone for its members. Now, what if an employee found something that could significantly improve the company or one of its departments, but would change the environment? That would be threatening. Such progress would push people outside their comfort zone, and therefore would meet substantial resistance.

I know from experience. At one point in my career, I was hired by a company to make significant changes in the way things were done, similar to major projects they knew I had done for other companies. At a meeting with the executive who hired me, he told me that it was very important that people were not made to feel uncomfortable. I asked to borrow his whiteboard and drew a circle signifying a comfort zone. I went through my explanation of this concept of the zone and showed that if I were to make significant changes, it would not only push the edges of people's comfort zone, but move them well outside the circle. If he wanted me to make substantial changes, he should be prepared: People would be made very uncomfortable.

Sometimes people use each other to help them avoid or mollify the discomfort of learning. For example, while a student at Hofstra University, I saw first-hand how some of my friends were trying to learn while maintaining themselves within a group comfort zone. I was studying in the library alone one day and this group of students was gathered together at a table. One of them, a good friend, asked me, "How did you do so well on your tests?" Without hesitation, I replied, "You are all sitting here trying to figure out what you need to know for the final exam. I am trying to figure out what I *don't* know.

As a group, they were actually limiting what they would learn by agreeing on which topics to discuss, which they thought would be relevant to the test. Individually, they were staying in their comfort zone, but they were further restricting themselves by keeping within the group's comfort zone. If each of them went off separately and studied part of the material alone, then came back together only for questions about the material, I wonder whether they would have stretched themselves much further. While a group can be useful for answering individual questions, it limits new territories of learning or experience.

Another factor that limits learning is the fear of making mistakes. You can't let mistakes affect your confidence; they must be viewed as trial-and-error learning experiences. Inevitably, whenever you venture into new experiences, you will have great difficulties and commit many errors. Doing something new and different also will very likely lead to criticism or cautions from all those who told you not to do it. Keep in mind: These experiences are most likely outside *their* comfort zone. Because it is outside their comfort zone, they will discourage venturing into it.

Here is where you face a major decision point. Do you want to spend your life in the same place, in the arms and comfort of those you have always known? If you do, you're done. There may be nothing wrong with just living in your current situation, if that is what you truly want as your final outcome.

However, accept that it was *you* who made that decision not to push into new territory. When you see somebody else who pushes themselves up from modest beginnings, don't resent them for having or doing more than you. They paid a significant price, pushing through some very uncomfortable parts of their life in order to attain their success. If you want to make similar progress, you have to understand that part of the cost will be significant periods of discomfort.

As an example of dealing with such discomfort, let's look at the challenge of learning the skill of snow skiing. In order to successfully ski downhill, your first experiences must be uncomfortable. You must put the body in a position that does not feel familiar. You lean downhill, which is counterintuitive to the way you would stand. It will feel odd. But if you don't do it, you will continue to fall on or at the moguls, if you ever get that far.

When we step back and think about it, the more progress we make, the more uncomfortable we will feel, at times. But once you do something new for a while and push through the introductory learning period, the more comfortable and normal this experience will feel. Don't worry about making errors; that's part of learning. But how you approach an error will determine your self-confidence. If you expect errors and try to minimize them, you will look at them as bumps in the road. It means you are learning to feel more comfortable with both the changes made as well as the process of changing things in your life. Remember the story about the first manned space shuttle to the moon. The flight was fraught with thousands of errors that needed to be continuously corrected. But nobody at NASA was depressed over the corrections; they expected them.

Another way to assuage the pain of making mistakes is to expand your comfort zone—before leaping out of it altogether. Think back to my experience taking the Dale Carnegie course to overcome my fear of public speaking. By putting myself in the safe environment provided by the course, I was able to learn the skill of public speaking, undeterred by the fear of looking foolish and performing poorly in front of people. And by the time I completed the course, I had stretched way outside my original comfort zone. I still look back and am amazed that in about 10 weeks, I went from a nervous person with no confidence to a good, comfortable speaker with tremendous confidence.

Stepping well outside our comfort zone can be painful and can be full of discouragement from those around us. So, how do we continue to do it against these seemingly endless odds. You need to start building that feeling that you "like feeling uncomfortable." Now, let me restate that in another way. Every time you step outside and are successful, you should understand and enjoy the success of whatever you did. Whether it is speaking in front of an audience or skiing down a mountain, it doesn't matter. You just had a success. As we know, success helps breed success. The more of these successes you have the more willing you will to be uncomfortable in other areas. So, it is really some of the early stages of jumping out of your comfort zone that are the hardest. It is also true that while you are outside, you will meet other people who are not only encouraging, but are doing the things outside your comfort zone, too.

When dealing with mentally challenging areas of life, such as studying for a new career, you will inevitably face times of great difficulties and setbacks—and your mind will want to take you on a vacation. All of the sudden you will feel very tired. You must fight that feeling. Understand that one of the reasons we are taught certain "proper" ways to sit while studying is because if we make the body too comfortable, we are most likely to fall asleep or at least feel tired and desire rest. We must grab onto our successes and use those to encourage us to continue to make progress.

Remember, one of the most difficult parts of reaching outside your comfort zone is that some of your current friends will probably not be there. Why? Because they'll start to feel uncomfortable as you expand your comfort zone to areas that are new to them. Also, your friends will naturally discourage you. You may and probably will lose some of them along the way. They may no longer feel included in your life, your schedule or there may be something else, like jealousy, at play. If they were true friends and wanted your success and the best for you, they would understand. But if not, you'll make new friends as you continue to grow. (This will be discussed much further in a later chapter on friends and family.)

Let's briefly recount an experience I talked about earlier in the book, when I was in the service and earning money from outside work—as much as I got from the service—but I was saving every cent. One day, a friend asked me, "Why are you saving? You may die tomorrow." I don't actually know whether he was questioning what I was doing, or feeling guilty that he was not doing the same thing himself. Whatever the reason, I immediately replied, "What happens if I live?" My friend was living for the present. That was a *comfortable* place to be. I was working on my future, which, because it is unknown and more uncertain, is definitely uncomfortable. How many times have you heard people say, "Live in the moment"? Of course, it's important to concentrate on what you are doing at the moment, but do not interpret that to mean you shouldn't be planning and working toward the future.

There is a problem when someone moves out of the comfort zone of their friends and it may be similar to resentment or feelings like, "Why not me"? How many times have you heard someone say, "I could have done that too?" Keep in mind that 80% of the "rich" started from poverty. They weren't given success. Most of what you are reading in this book are the very actions they have taken.

If you have any remaining doubt about how a comfort zone can limit your life, look at some dying city or town. In almost every instance, a large number of people will not move because they say, "This is my home." Does it make sense that someone would remain in a place with little or no hope? Well, that is an individual choice. I can't say that it is right or wrong, but it is a clear example of the effect of somebody's comfort zone restricting themselves and the comfort zones of their friends, family and neighbors affecting them.

When you fully understand the effect of cohesiveness on a dying city or town, you can also reflect on what this does to people in inner cities. How can we expect people to make progress when they spend all of their time among others with the same problems and experiences? During the big real estate boom in center cities, social critics started screaming about poor people being pushed out of their homes and neighborhoods being broken up. These people were being forced to move to the outskirts, borderline suburbs, for more affordable housing. Now, the people screaming were truly thinking about what they felt was best for the poor. At that time, I pointed out that while people were uncomfortable with the transition, it was ultimately beneficial to force greater assimilation into society. Progress needs us to break out of the binds of our comfort zone.

Like a dying city, the same is true for a dying art or an enterprise left behind by new technologies. These entities no longer make economic sense, despite the support of workers or politicians who stubbornly resist breaking out of their comfort zone. Some people are fighting inevitability with programs such as "buy local" programs without making a strong economic and competitive reason for the consumer.

Also, think of all the majors or specialties that college students choose because they like it or have a "passion" for it—without regard to a future with the job market. None of these students should complain when they can't find a job. If they want to be happy in a field that pays little or nothing, that is their choice. If nobody wants to pay them well for the career with limited demand or an oversupply of eager potential employees, I hope they get some other satisfaction from it. I often have this discussion with people—usually women—who study social work.

That returns us to the path of dreaming and setting goals for where we truly want to go. After we properly and thoroughly set these goals, our task is to determine how we will get there, overcoming the discomfort of making necessary changes. And it often doesn't end there, as we raise or change our goals during most of our life.

12

Change Your Perspective of Yourself

'You only live once, but if you do it right, once is enough'

~ Mae West

Self-image is the perspective you have of yourself. It's the inner voice you need to remove self-doubts, reduce lack of confidence and accept and recognize compliments. To improve, to change, to grow—these are all things that will only be realized after you believe in yourself. That is, you must have a new self-image. You want to walk tall and attract successful people and opportunities. Think about it: How are you going to develop and gain the confidence to take on new adventures if your inner voice doesn't believe you can?

Changing how you look at yourself is an ongoing process. Expect it to be slow; it's not a switch that can be flipped. I'm not talking literally about how you look every day—if you like working from home in your pajamas or sweats all day, that's fine. Dress in a way that makes you feel good when you look in the mirror—although most experts recommend that you will actually feel better and be more productive if you "dress for work," even if casually, if you are working from home.

Whether reversing negative perceptions or increasing and enhancing a positive perspective on your abilities, developing your self-image is a process that needs constant nurturing, learning and exposure to new things and to new people. The people around you greatly influence the self esteem you have. Changing many of these things is part of personal growth. To achieve a strong self-image, you need successes, building self-confidence as you create a better picture and outlook for yourself. Yes, we all know we have flaws and sometimes many, (see Chapter 4, about overcoming weaknesses), but your image must develop into where you are going and not where you have been or are.

All this requires a purposeful plan to gain knowledge, increase talents, skills, will and determination. My own self-image developed substantially while I was in the military, when two things came together for me. As I related in my introduction, I was given inspirational advice by several mentors and was able to complete a significant challenge and attitude—Russian language school—when previously I never believed I could learn a much simpler language like German. And the thought occurred to me: If the military could get me to do something this far beyond my expectations for *their* purposes, I could take that same energy, will, perseverance and determination to help myself grow into new areas that would build my future. This time, it would be for me.

Now, it's your time. Short of joining the military, you need to find motivators to inspire you to complete something beyond what you thought you could do. Here, we are only looking at how you need to change your self-perspective, but your approach should be similar to what I've proposed previously: break down goals into smaller pieces. Why? You need to build little successes that build your confidence. Choose from among your weaknesses or some target you are trying to attain. Break it down into reasonable goals. As you succeed with each partial goal, you build the confidence to move to the next. Because my environment and the people around me changed while in the military, many of my "outside" negative influences were no longer present.

As an example, let's look again at the goal of learning to speak in front of a group, which many people (including me) have realized we need to do. Public speaking has many components: nervousness, outline and preparation, how to research a topic, appearance, and a little bit of acting. There are many people who are good at the job and knowledgeable about the topic they present. They still may need to learn how to outline and prepare for a speech and believe in their ability to charm an audience, or they will be very nervous. For me, the Dale Carnegie course I referred to earlier was the first step I took to greatly help me overcome nervousness and gain confidence. In many other instances, breaking down the final goal into smaller pieces and overcoming one at a time increases not only success, but confidence as well. Confidence-building enables and yields the strong, positive self-image.

Self-confidence also can be bolstered by understanding where you are relative to others—not as a comparison instilling jealousy, but rather the opportunity to put your own weaknesses in perspective. For example, I've heard that Bob Hope was extremely nervous before every performance—almost to the point of being sick. If that happened to Bob Hope, who entertained millions of people around the world, what makes the rest of us think we're above getting nervous? Too often, the confidence someone else exudes creates fear within us that we might not be able to perform as well. Then we learn about Bob Hope's nervousness; that puts everything into perspective.

If you care enough about being the best you can be, it's quite natural to be nervous until you get started. In fact, if you *don't* feel nervous, you should be concerned, because your mental trigger to aim for success and true excellence is probably not there. Nervousness, as successful performers like Hope demonstrated, was just part of their intensity. Being cavalier was not an option. Ultimately, this helped make success more achievable for me because I was always extremely nervous before speaking in public.

When I learned that this was natural for the greatest speakers, I focused on just starting—and being well prepared.

In addition, it is often important to change your environment while putting time and energy into developing new skills to build self-confidence. That created a great opportunity for me when I was in the military. This is what I did as I went back to college—I decided to postpone or give up a social life to focus on a new level of intellectual challenges. I applied this idea after college, avoiding the habit of watching new TV programs that would take away from the time I needed to grow. There is only so much time in each day, and if I was going to gain new skills, I needed to harness as much of that time as possible. I not only needed to study, but gain new skills. The world of business and employment is competitive. If you have a dozen candidates or businessmen that 2 years ago were all equal, but one of them spent 20 % more time learning skills, who would you expect to win the business or job? Relate that to yourself. Your future in 2, 5, or 10 years will depend on what you do in the meantime.

While reconsidering your environment, this is also a good time to evaluate your "friends." Continue to develop your good friends, while cleaning out your closet of negative people. When you share one of your accomplishments with a friend—or someone you believe is your friend—does that person support it and encourage you, or respond with sarcasm or jokes and put down the accomplishment? If they do the latter, it doesn't matter what else they do for you. They are lowering your self-esteem and holding you back. When my consultant company was at its peak, one of my closest friends would question me negatively. While it annoyed me at the time, I had so much success at the time it didn't really affect me. But during tough times, those same negative comments would be devastating. Why? While you don't have the confidence or strength in your conviction, you are vulnerable. Remove those folks from your life.

Avoid peer pressure. Note: I did not say, "Do not succumb to peer pressure." Not succumbing to peer pressure would mean that you have to continually address it, perhaps hanging around friends who want to go out or watch TV. It's hard to continually say, "No I don't feel like doing that." Soon, you'll seem argumentative. There is no need to make announcements about what you're doing or where you are going. When I was in school, I avoided peer pressure by finding and staying in an isolated spot in the library. Then, if someone said, "Let's go somewhere"—unless it was time that was already intended for a break—I would say something enthusiastically, like, "Let me meet you later; I have to do something first. Where are you going to be and I'll come by after I'm done?" That way, I could be both direct, honest and diplomatic, maintaining my study plan while acknowledging the camaraderie of friends—as long as the needs of both schedules could be reasonably met.

Keep yourself in a positive atmosphere, with mentors or other people who are working hard to attain the goals you want. This may mean you will be making new friends and spending less time with some of your older friends. Hang on to mental images of positive times to reinforce your ability to make progress. (More on peers and family in Chapter 16.)

In a broad sense, changing your perspective means breaking old habits and making new habits. To develop a habit, you do something over and over, until it is so familiar that it becomes normal practice. It's very much like exercise. It must be done gradually and consistently in order for you to see the results and have them last. You are developing a new habit—and a new confidence.

As we discussed previously, when we move outside our comfort zone, it means by definition that we are doing something both uncomfortable and difficult. We are not just talking about gently pushing against the envelope, but rather moving well outside it. But if we have broken our goal that is well outside our comfort zone into sufficiently small pieces, each piece or mini-goal may be no more than pushing slightly outward on the envelope.

I continue to rail against that common expression, "pushing the envelope." Imagine where you would like to be and then imagine just pushing against the envelope. In effect you have all the factors and "friends" inside your comfort zone that are holding on to you. You need to find that isolated or new environment and throw yourself out there in order to accelerate your progress. Pushing the envelope will take lifetimes to truly reach "breakthrough success."

So, as you develop greater confidence with your broader comfort zone, you become more confident with a better perspective of yourself. With this greater confidence and repeated success outside your comfort zone, the improved perspective of yourself allows you to feel comfortable making progress and that is being outside your comfort zone. In other words, you can feel comfortable being uncomfortable.

Finally, while outside factors will inevitably affect you, don't let them disrupt your plan. In order to do this and maintain your focus, you must reduce your stress level. That means eating well, exercising and trying to stay healthy. Exercise may only be 30 minutes at the gym each day. It may be nothing more than a strong morning walk. The key is consistency, truly exercising, not just going out for a stroll. It will keep your mind fresh and help you gain confidence with your life and goals. And while it's easy to do, such consistent practice is one way to find a daily opening toward success.

13
Learning the Skill of Self-Motivation

'Self Trust is the first secret of success'

~ Ralph Waldo Emerson

Some people simply have a zest for life. They seem to have complete self-motivation and self-confidence. At the same time, there are others who say, "Maybe someone will appear and 'turn me on.'" (Of course, they don't consider what happens if that person doesn't show up.) Then there are the majority of people who fall between these two types: They would like to be more self-motivated but either they don't know how, are influenced by others, or are afraid of being disappointed, so they don't try. Now, while motivation—that which drives us to a goal—seems rather simple, self-motivation is a key to personal development and relies on emotional factors. These factors include personal drive, discipline to maintain progress toward a goal, ability to react and act on impediments or opportunities, and attitude—in an optimistic sense.

Self-motivation is one of the most difficult practices to learn and maintain. It both leads to—and comes from—increased self-confidence. So we have a proverbial chicken-and-egg question: Which comes first, self-confidence or self-motivation? In this chapter, I've decided to focus on self-motivation, the skill to push yourself into new experiences outside your comfort zone, because you cannot expect to have self-confidence in something you have never done previously. While learning the skill to motivate others is also a difficult task, you first need to learn the skill to motivate yourself, overcoming the onslaught of negative thoughts from within yourself, as well as from those around you who doubt your abilities.

How can you improve this skill of self-motivation? And yes, it *is* a skill that can be developed. It does not occur naturally. You can't expect anyone to "turn you on"—more likely, they will turn you off.

As noted in our previous chapter on setting goals the first 18 to 23 years of a person's life are largely motivated by short-range goals set by others, with precise timing and rewards or disappointments. Whether it was your parents determining whether you were allowed to do something, or your teachers determining when an exam was scheduled and what you were expected to know for it, or some part-time job where you were given specific instructions, these were outside forces. You did not explicitly motivate yourself. You may have pushed yourself to complete the work, but you did not necessarily assign the reward or punishment for not completing it.

As with goal-setting, building self-motivation requires you to create a well-thought-out plan, but also constant performance incentives and challenges while you potentially adjust these goals. You must have a strong desire and a determined focus for each step in your goals. In order to motivate yourself and sustain your drive for the work you are engaged in, you need to break the work into small chunks, each of which can represent something you have completed—adding up to a series of mini-successes that will build confidence.

As an example of a major project, let's take fixing up the backyard, which can consist of many tasks: mowing the lawn, trimming the bushes, weeding the garden, cleaning off the porch or patio, cleaning the fence and fertilizing the lawn. If you think of this project as one large task, you might be severely disappointed if you didn't complete it—anything less than finishing it would make you feel unaccomplished. But if you think of the project in terms of the six specific tasks, you can feel a sense of accomplishment as you complete each one, which will keep you motivated and provide encouragement to continue with the project.

I've had this experience throughout various periods of my own life. When I was in graduate school, for instance, I found that researching and writing a dissertation normally takes about two years. Without breaking the dissertation into relatively small pieces, it would have been nearly impossible for me to complete.

This approach has continued though my daily life today, in regular projects such as taking care of my lawn. Many of my neighbors have often complimented me about "what a great lawn" I have, and I'm sure they wonder how I have the time to spend on it. For them, the problem is that they have made lawn care into a monumental, time-consuming task, so it never gets done well. I, on the other hand, have broken the monumental task into many mini-tasks, almost all of them doable in 15 to 30 minutes: spot-weeding, trimming, bug spraying, fertilizing, applying lime. Only the mowing may take 40 minutes. So every task I finish is an accomplishment that feeds into my "successes."

As you work through various tasks, you should keep track of your progress. Tracking progress not only keeps you moving forward, but acts as motivation that will aid your confidence when times get tough. If you remember that you managed to complete some difficult tasks or projects, you can hold onto that as inspiration to help you break through something tough the next time around. You are developing a positive attitude—self-confidence—based on strength. Over time, this aura of self-confidence will assist you in breaking new ground, learning new skills and becoming a person with a can-do attitude to take on and complete new challenges. You will start enjoying life outside the comfort zone.

So the very process of breaking a goal into small tasks will help provide you with self-confidence, which is a major factor in self-motivation to complete every new task. In effect, you have built yourself a little system of many potential successes. At the same time, however, you also need to think about the potential negative consequences of *not* completing your agenda—similar to the concept of "Why not?" in Chapter 7—what happens when you do not reach your goals. The degree to which you are motivated by negative consequences or positive consequences is something that only you, alone, can fully evaluate. This is a big jump from the never ending excuses of your earlier behavior, like middle school whining, blame and jealousy. You may be someone who is so used to making and accepting your own excuses, and who is so comfortable with not getting things done, that developing self-motivation will be especially difficult. If you are someone who isn't bothered by not completing tasks, you may need to concentrate on developing this skill. That is, to be able to visualize a negative consequence to not completing a task just like you knew something would happen if you didn't do your homework or study for a test when you were younger.

It's also important to avoid negative people who could encourage you to fall off task. You will increase your chances of staying motivated if you surround yourself with like-minded people. Think of it as developing team spirit. During the learning and confidence-building period, your ego is fragile, easily influenced by others. You will need to build relationships that nurture growth and change. Those relationships, as you will see in a future chapter, may not be with the same friends, family or colleagues with whom you are now spending time.

Deadlines often serve a useful purpose: They mark both the end of a task and pressure us to complete it. Many people are not highly motivated until the deadline is upon them. Some have trouble focusing on a task until they enter a state of near panic. While they may claim that they perform best under the pressure of a deadline, usually this means they cannot focus until the deadline is upon them. If they could focus with laser-like vision and they had more time for a project, I believe it would be fair to say that the quality of their work would be higher. How could they maintain this increased focus for longer periods of time? Once again, by designing the project as a series of small tasks, creating their own mini-deadlines along the way.

At the same time, we all need to build some slack time into our plans. A family emergency might arise, or you might become ill, or some other minor incident might emerge, any of which could interrupt your plan for a short period of time. Buffer time allows you to catch up or keep up even when life presents you with interruptions. For example, while in college, I realized that I could easily catch a cold and that could set me back a week. During a short semester, if you fell behind by a week, there was little time to catch up, especially if you were striving toward a high level of achievement. So before the semester began, I would give myself a head start by working on each of the books in my curriculum. This meant that I was always using this slack time to review material before classes, rather than seeing it for the first time during class. If something still wasn't clear to me, I was not embarrassed to ask a clarification question. That was far better than either asking some question that showed that I was not prepared, or waiting until the end of the semester and attempting to catch up on material I missed because I had been sick and fell behind.

Generally, as you complete tasks, you want to focus on positive outcomes, which can include creating rewards that will be pleasing, satisfying, and fulfilling. Reward yourself at the end, and determine ahead of time what the reward will be. Before I finished a draft of this chapter, for example, I decided beforehand that I would go down to the waterfront for a nice walk and look at the shops; I was sure I would get it done.

Your rewards do not have to be big. I discovered this when I was in college and maintained a strict schedule, supported by a series of small breaks. For each hour I spent in the classroom, I spent three hours studying on my own—some wisdom I learned from a book about how to study. Additionally, I wanted to make sure that during the half hour before each class, I would be able to review what would be taught that day. Within two hours of the end of each class, I would quickly review my notes from class.
om the class. To accomplish all of this, I realized that I would have little spare time. So I mapped out my day into two-hour increments, with each two-hour period divided into an hour and 50 minutes of intense study and a 10-minute break. During that break, I would stand up from my desk, maybe take a short walk, grab

a snack or even do a household chore like dusting a room, cleaning the kitchen counters and doing dishes. These chores are what I refer to as "brain-dead tasks," and because they were unrelated to my academic work, they briefly took my mind off studies.

Those 10-minute breaks may not seem like a big deal, but they actually produced two very satisfying rewards. They gave me relief from heavy study, as well as a deadline by which to complete a task within a tight time frame. Furthermore, I felt good about completing chores that I would otherwise have had to do during my limited free time. When I was done with work, I was indeed free.

Break times can be used as rewards, as well as a buffer against unexpected problems. You may be able to schedule short breaks into your daily life—or for major projects, complete mornings, afternoons or whole days. Now you have two potential options going for you. If you schedule one free day each week, you can have a nice one-day reward, or you can have a day to catch up. How should you choose to use it? Whatever your decision, it becomes another motivator to get the job done. Remember, the day off is not an obligation that must be taken, but a reward for having completed tasks on time. If you don't reward yourself at least a little, you will eventually feel as if you are not receiving anything for completing your tasks. Anyone can push very hard for a short period of time, but maintaining a high level of performance wears a person down, if not rewarded.

Thus, self-motivation becomes an effective tool for increasing our skills not so much by shoving us forward, but rather attracting us to what we can accomplish next. As we overcome challenges and our satisfaction develops, we recognize our own achievements. The act of actually completing the tasks becomes a pleasurable experience that we train ourselves to repeat.

As you move through the process of completing both short- and long-term goals always keep a written copy of your plans close at hand. Monitor your progress; pay attention to how you're moving. It's fine if you have an opportunity to get ahead of schedule, but don't aim to overachieve. You can reevaluate your goals, but keep them reasonable, achievable, and a realistic fit for your life. One or two great days don't mean that every day will be great, and the speed at which you complete a long-term goal or mission is not nearly as important as having completed it according to the schedule that you established.

The greater goal here is to teach yourself to become someone who is motivated by completing tasks. Self-motivation leads to repeated successes, which, in turn, sets you up for further accomplishments and more successful goal-setting in the future, and ultimately, a growing sense of self-confidence.

14

Understand and Reduce Procrastination

'Do the hard jobs first. The easy jobs will take care of themselves.'
– Dale Carnegie

Have you ever found yourself trying to repair an appliance in your house—a task that seemed so overwhelming that you decided to take on a far easier option, like washing the dishes? Or have you ever decided to apply for a job, but spent so much time continually refining your résumé that by the time you were ready, the job was filled? Or have you ever called in sick to avoid a deadline or an exam? Crammed for a test or done your homework the night before it was due, even though you had a week to do it?

On any given day, we all procrastinate to some degree. Often, we are not aware of it, as we fill our time with nonessential busywork. Whenever we delay working on a task that is somewhat uncomfortable—

writing, for example—in favor of doing something else that is more comfortable or enjoyable to work on, we are procrastinating. So here we find ourselves again, as we discovered two chapters ago—encountering the challenge of staying in our "comfort zone."

Procrastination can interfere with our goals, our careers, even the simple daily activities in which we want to excel, or even hobbies or sports. Procrastination can become a habit and, unfortunately, it is self-reinforcing. Left untreated, procrastination will spread throughout your life, like a cancer. Granted, you're not going to die from procrastination. On the other hand, you can get successful treatments for cancer and eventually become declared cancer-free, whereas you're not likely to ever be procrastination-free in your lifetime.

The first difficulty in facing down procrastination is recognizing it. Procrastination comes in many forms, not only choosing desirable tasks over undesirable ones. Most people just think of procrastination as watching TV or engaging in some other fun instead of doing something that is necessary. If you choose to bypass important jobs or chores that you really need to complete for less important ones, that, too, is procrastination. Of course, you should dust the rooms in the house, iron the clothes, and weed the yard, but not in place of more important tasks. This can be especially problematic for a self-employed individual at home, who may find it much easier to do these tasks than making the phone calls or doing the paperwork necessary to generate business growth. So procrastination can easily disguise itself as still being productive, doing all the little unnecessary things that are more comfortable than what you should be focusing on.

But the most common idea on procrastination also comes in a more blatant form. Sometimes it is nothing more than postponing important tasks, assuming that you can complete them later, and using the current time instead for recreational activities. Think about the occasions, whether in school or at work, that a project or report was due by a specific deadline—not immediately but rather in a week or a month. Have you ever waited until the last minute? When you do little to finish a project until the pressure is intense, you have procrastinated.

Procrastination can also come in the form of trying to control or perfect a project, before it is even under way. If you are planning, discussing, and dreaming about its outcome but not taking action, you may be procrastinating. Planning is necessary, but *over-planning* becomes avoidance.

How do we fight procrastination?

We have to change the habits that enable procrastination—and this may be a lifelong task, because we break a habit only when we consistently stop doing it. We need to search for as many ways as possible to change our habits of procrastination. Some corrective actions will work better than others, depending on the individual. While not every method is going to work for all of us, each of us needs to make a consistent effort to change our habits.

To counter procrastination when working on important tasks, you need substantial self-motivation. Any large project may appear overwhelming and be difficult to fit into your schedule. You usually need dedicated, uninterrupted time. Once again, we return to the issue of self-motivation—and making up your own rewards to spur you complete a major task. You need to experience a warm feeling of accomplishment that will reinforce the completion of each part of a task. Make sure you truly understand how it feels to finish a task—the completion, itself, becomes a positive experience. It is only after repeatedly having that experience that you can break your habits of procrastination. If you have broken the job or work into smaller, well-defined tasks, you have the benefit of that feeling of accomplishment many times.

Conversely, when you don't accomplish a task, identify the feeling and consequences of that failure. Then use this negative image to help you work through the rough spots in the future. (Recall the chapter, "Why not?" We're using the same principle here. You are building an arsenal of undesirable images to motivate you away from failure.)

As noted in the last chapter, when you divide a task into smaller steps, you accomplish several things. First, bite-size pieces are easier to complete. Second, many small, positive experiences of completion, combined with the positive experience of completing the task overall, become reinforcing behavior and decrease your tendency to procrastinate. This process will increase the probability that the overall task will actually get finished. If the task was left as one big project, anything less than completion of the entire project would be considered minimally as undone and very likely as a failure. Remember the example of achieving excellent lawn care while everyone around me failed by trying too much at once. They wondered why their lawn was a failure.

Furthermore, by breaking a project into small pieces—each with finite amount of time to be completed—you can create a sense of urgency with each task. For example, when I was writing this book I set aside small chunks of time in which to complete certain tasks. For each chapter, I developed an outline. I would allocate one hour to work on progressing from my notes to an outline. That was a fairly tight schedule. But the satisfaction that came from completion and making progress reinforced my success which, in turn, helped me avoid procrastination on subsequent chapters. For writing a draft of a chapter, I allocated two hours. If I found myself starting to fall behind schedule, I forced myself to concentrate harder and push to finish the job.

My experience with writing is no different from that of a student faced with the looming prospect of not studying sufficiently and rushing to finish an essay or report. What I did, however, was to manage the pressure that usually arises as the due date for a project draws near: With the project broken into small pieces, each step of it had its own share of pressure that would motivate me to complete it within the specified time frame. By the end of the project, I had invested sufficient time into each piece. My confidence and motivation was increased when I saw the completion of each smaller piece.

Sometimes procrastination results from the disorganization in your life. When you do anything that requires concentration, it's not easy to focus when you are surrounded by a mess. Granted, some people claim they can concentrate under such conditions. I only wonder if their performance would improve if their surroundings were organized.

Similarly, to get a job done well, you must focus completely on the task at hand. Multitasking may work if you are trying to accomplish tasks like certain household chores, errands, or busywork, which you can do even when you're tired. But if you are using the time you need for your important tasks to take care of the little things that "need to be done," you are really just procrastinating.

When you focus on the task at hand, anything that might distract you should be pushed aside. It doesn't matter whether the task is an academic lesson, a work project or physical exercise: Focus only on what you're doing. One trick to assist you in maintaining focus is to always have a pad and pen near you, even when you are sleeping. If your brain wants to wander, just jot down the thought on a piece of paper and return to it later. Even if the task you're doing is so simple that you understand it completely, resist the impulse to let your mind drift off or multitask. Instead, use any spare brainpower to think of the underpinnings or causality of what you are doing, or what is being discussed in the book you are reading, or of the lecture you are hearing.

How many times have you seen people sending or reading text messages or e-mail when listening to a lecture? In a recent talk I gave, I mentioned an occasion when I was participating as a speaker at a training program. I was off to the side while another presenter was speaking, and I pointed out to a colleague next to me that there was only one person in the entire session taking notes. Why were these people even there?

Something I learned from my champion power builder friend, Joe, many years ago is useful in all situations: If you are exercising, think about and concentrate on the muscle being exercised. The mind helps ensure not only that you are using that muscle for the exercise but also that you are using it properly. Yes, that means that you should stop multitasking—such as reading magazines or studying your lecture notes—while you're on the treadmill, stationary bike or elliptical.

One of the best ways to fight procrastination is to become a master at scheduling and project planning. You need to develop a strong and realistic understanding of time, allocating periods for breaks as well as busywork or brainless tasks. With a good, tight schedule, you will be able to focus on the task at hand

and you will not have the time to procrastinate. For example, I put my necessary but "busy-work," such as filling out forms, paying bills, sending out notes, in my "brain dead time," which for me is after dinner. So, if this is a weakness, it is also one that can easily be learned and is necessary to overcome.

Often, when a new idea or task comes to mind, you may feel an immediate need to take some action toward addressing it. For example, if you're sitting in front of your computer and an e-mail message arrives, or if you receive a text message or phone call, you feel the urge to respond. One way to fight this urge is to mute the sounds from your electronic devices. Again, it's a good idea to keep a to-do list and a pen by your side in case something pops into mind, so you can jot it down and return to it later. That way, it is essentially out of mind, and you don't have to worry about forgetting it. Keep a pen and paper by your bed, too, in case you think of something during the night and worry that you'll forget it before morning. That often keeps you awake. Now you can write in down, relax and go back to sleep.

Prioritize your projects, tasks and chores. On your to-do list, rate each item with an A, B, or C, based on how important it is. In graduate school, one time while I was visiting my dissertation professor, he was sorting inbound mail into three folders. He explained that the C items were ones that he deemed unimportant and that he may never get to, but they were tentative and he wasn't ready to throw them out yet. The A items were ones that needed to be done immediately. In folder B was everything else. This is the same approach that you should use with your to-do list. Notice how so much I have learned was nothing more than listening and implementing the wisdom of others.

It also may be useful to work with an "accountability partner." Ask someone else to regularly check up on you and review your projects and scheduling process. (You would do the same for them.) In effect, you are creating your own peer pressure in order to get things done. This is actually the type of system used in various types of businesses, where somebody might be an accountability partner and is used in Mastermind Groups.

In general, most projects that you haven't had time to do for a long time will not affect your life. They are extras that can be done when you really do have the time—which may never actually happen. For example, you may have accumulated a pile of magazines or journals, and they may even be related to your work, but you just can't seem to find the time to look through them. You may feel it is important to watch the news on television so that you are aware of current events, but you never seem to have the time to do so. Prioritize these tasks honestly.

It is also important not to waste valuable time, just to finish something you already know is not worth the effort. I have always wondered, for instance, why people will sit through a movie at a theater, even after they realize within the first 10 minutes that it is terrible. They realize that they have wasted their money, but why are they now wasting their time, too? Cash in your time for something better. There are also times you will procrastinate simply because you find certain tasks or projects to be unpleasant. But generally, people overestimate the unpleasantness of a task. Even if a task is truly unpleasant, hold onto the mental picture of the consequence of *not* finishing the task. Of course, you will also have a mental picture of completing it.

For me, a good example is writing. I don't really like to write, partly because I tend to be a perfectionist. I will never be satisfied with my writing, so it is a painful process to watch the words appear on the screen and to constantly second-guess them. When writing, I keep in mind the quote from George Bernard Shaw, the great Irish writer, and the renowned economist, John Kenneth Galbraith, both of whom are credited with having said something like, "The only good thing about writing is having completed it." If those two prolific writers found writing painful, I thought, "I should accept that it is a difficult process and continue to push forward in order to complete my work in a reasonable period of time." So I adopt the strategy of breaking the book into several pieces, each chapter divided into several steps. Additionally, I read some books by well-known authors on the process of writing a book. They helped me change my perspective and taught me new steps to follow. Rather than worrying about the grammar or content or style of a particular chapter as I was writing it, I would focus on getting it done in order to have the time later to rewrite and make it better. If I failed to finish the chapter quickly, I would never have the opportunity to hone it.

So you see, there are a number of key points to keep in mind about procrastination: You need to be honest with yourself when you are pushing an important task aside or delaying working on it. Yes, recognize and admit to your own procrastination. Next, you need to break down a big project into small bites. Then, each bite needs to be assigned a tight, but reasonable, time schedule. That tight schedule will allow you to use the pressure that usually builds with an approaching due date to help you complete each step of the project. Don't forget to actually schedule some extra time for review, testing or checking to give you the opportunity to tune or add material that would not fit in the original schedule. That extra scheduled time helps prevent possible anxiety over not completing fully a task.

Consistently completing the tiny bites not only means that the entire project will get done, but it also creates a sense of satisfaction that comes from completing uncomfortable tasks, and it helps eliminate the general habit of procrastination. Most of all, recognize that, yes, you procrastinate. So do I. Let's just minimize procrastination and continually reinforce positive actions to counter it.

Chapter 15

Yoku Mimin Suru – Copy Well

'Master What the Master Has Already Done'
~ *Thomas O'Grady, PhD*

There are two ways to learn: The first is from our own experiences and mistakes; the second is from other people's experiences and mistakes. Almost everyone has heard or seen on TV the concept of leverage in investments, such as real estate, to increase your money or investment by using "Other People's Money," usually referred to as OPM. You use OPM because you don't have all the investment resources you would like on your own, so you work with other individuals or financial institutions to gain access to investment opportunities that you otherwise wouldn't have.

Similarly, there is not enough time in life to learn everything we all need to know, and we should use the analogy of OPM to apply it Other People's Experiences—let's call it OPE. In this case, we're leveraging OPE, and we're doing it interest-free.

Whenever possible, we're advised to learn from other people's experiences with credos such as, "Don't reinvent the wheel." This approach can be used in many areas, whether we are talking about acquiring wisdom or knowledge, as discussed in Part 1. Nevertheless, most people seem to ignore that approach and do the exact opposite—they attempt to reinvent things that already exist. While our pride and ignorance often seem to dominate our behavior when we're confronted with learning something new, what I am proposing here is to use the tried-and-true practice of copying the success of others: Invest in your future by using OPE—Other People's Experiences.

Different cultures are known for excelling at certain practices, and the Japanese, in particular, are known for copying success. In Japanese, *Yoku mimin suru* means, "You copy well." To maintain its strong culture and society, Japan has long relied on the conformity and consistency of its people. Granted, conformity restricts creativity. At the same time, an individual's overzealous pride in doing something "creatively"—his or her own way—can restrict growth and prevents consistency. Because of the Japanese pride in copying well, the country greatly benefits in its manufacturing sector, where products are made with tremendous consistency and quality. The country does suffer in the area of creativity, but the Japanese have learned much from the process of carefully copying others, and only after mastering the re-creation of something do they become innovative, enhancing or improving an original design. I believe that copying should be one of the easiest skills you ever develop. Yet, copying well—that is, *precisely*—appears to be one of the most difficult skills, based on the failures I've seen from people trying to duplicate even the simplest successes.

Let's take a closer look at how successful the Japanese have become by copying well. They have done this in many industries. They first did it in stereo receivers and electronics where the Germans had the best products. They also copied watches from Switzerland and then cameras from Germany. (Yes, Germany was the premier maker of cameras before Japan.) Japan's automotive industry provides a strong modern-day example, though we could look at their production of cameras, watches or electronics, too.

The Japanese took the lead in the automotive industry by first copying the assembly-line process. They broke down the assembly process of an automobile into small steps. They built a manufacturing system around the principle of making certain that every step was simplified and precisely repeatable. They copied the technology and work processes and maintained them until they were completely confident in the systems as they currently existed. They thoroughly trained, tracked and measured their employees on precisely repeated, known processes. Only after succeeding at producing nearly perfect copies—that is, within small tolerances—did Japanese manufacturers devote their efforts to improving individual pieces of the vehicle itself and advancing the manufacturing process—which would not have been possible if they had not first copied well. Using this methodology, they were able to achieve incredible results with incredible speed. How much faster can you develop something if you just copy a success, rather than start with a "clean slate"? How much faster can you improve something if you limit your focus only on improvements and not what is already done?

In America, we pride ourselves on our creativity. While it is a great blessing, it is also a curse. Because of our strong roots in creative, innovative endeavors, Americans' pride gets in the way and we generally struggle with copying success precisely. I see this struggle on an almost daily basis and marvel at it every time. I can hand somebody a set of instructions involving three or four simple steps, then later, listen to him explain how the process "didn't quite work." When I ask him what he did, he describes his attempt, but not the precise instructions. I repeat the description of the process, and he says, "That's just what I did." Yet when I ask him again exactly what he did, his description is clearly not the same. When I point out this difference and ask whether he understands, the response I get is, "Well, sort of." (At this point, I wonder what I should say openly, since what's going through my mind cannot be said out loud!)

One great story I love to share about the challenges of copying success precisely comes from a former general manager at Chevrolet who became a friend of mine when he worked at Toyota, heading the

Lexus division. One day several years ago I was talking to him about the topic of copying when he laughed and said that he had his own story I had to hear. We were at a press function, so we went out of earshot of others. He told me about an engineer in charge of fixing the oil pan on the brand-new Chevy Cavalier. The oil pan had a leak. It was supposed to be an exact copy of the Honda Accord oil pan—*that* one certainly didn't leak. He went to the engineer and asked how it could leak if it was an exact copy of the Accord oil pan. He told the engineer to get it fixed.

In about two weeks, my friend went back to see the engineer and asked how the oil pan repair was coming along. The engineer pulled out drawings and covered the table with diagrams that showed how he was designing the oil pan. My friend again explained the engineer that this is supposed to be an exact copy of the Honda Accord oil pan: "Just copy it."

A couple weeks later my friend again met with the engineer. Much to his amazement, the engineer was still trying to design a new oil pan. Let's just say that my friend, the general manager, expressed his displeasure thoroughly. Think about how much time and work was wasted on such an unnecessary endeavor. And imagine how much better off we'd be if we not let our pride get in the way and just copy success and use our creative abilities to improve products, to improve marketing, to better position products, and to come up with new products faster by using existing components where appropriate.

The same can be said for everything we learn. That is, don't try to reinvent what already exists. Don't redo what is already done well. Advance your own knowledge by finding a mentor or someone who is successful in whatever you desire and follow his or her process and instructions precisely. Do not put your own spin on it until you become a master at it. *Master what the master has already done!*

One of my best personal examples of copying success *precisely* relates to physical exercise. You may remember from an earlier chapter the story about my friend, Joe, a champion power lifter, who had won the Texas, Oklahoma, and New Mexico heavyweight divisions of the tri-state power lifting championship. When I met Joe I was a skinny 19-year-old kid, 6 feet 3 inches and 162 pounds. Several years earlier, I had tried to gain weight. After reading a newspaper article that noted that the players on the Green Bay Packers football team consumed over 5,000 calories per day during training camp, I proceeded to eat over 6,000 calories per day. After six weeks, I lost one pound.

At the time, my knees were hurting so Joe offered to help me exercise, saying that if I built up some muscle, my knees would have better support and I'd feel better. We exercised together and ate together. He told me exactly how to exercise, when to do it, how to breathe, how to concentrate, and much more. One time, he noticed me looking at two guys who I thought were in really good shape. I was thinking, "Wow, I hope I can get to their level." Joe stopped me and said, "Don't look at anyone else. Concentrate on yourself and what you are doing. You will pass them in about six weeks."

He was correct. I had started exercising with him at the end of the second week in September. On December 24, within just three months and one week from the day I had started, I had gone from 162 pounds down to 158 pounds but then up to 190 pounds. When people saw me, almost everyone I knew asked me what I had done to gain the muscle mass. As I explained in my chapter on goals, I was able to achieve goals I had previously not thought possible because I had a mentor whose wisdom I respected. But on top of that, I was willing to copy well—to do *exactly* as I was told, following Joe's instructions without challenging his direction. He was truly a master; I would have been quite a fool not to do exactly what he told me.

While in graduate school studying for my Ph.D., I went back to exercising based on exactly what Joe taught me—this time just to relieve stress of an incredibly rigorous academic program. I didn't intend to get very big, physically, but again, I followed Joe's instructions precisely. I never exercised for more than 40 minutes. Yet I became second biggest in a large California gym. Over the next few years, many people in the gyms where I worked out asked me to show them what I did. I offered several of them the chance to exercise with me, one at a time. I was glad to share what I had learned, but unfortunately, every one of them found excuses to miss a couple of sessions or felt it was too hard. They soon quit. Success requires work, and work separates those who do from those who only dream. But can be much easier when you put your trust in the mentor and start by copying exactly—something these people could not do. You have to ask yourself, "Am I willing to put in the effort to succeed?" Think back to the concepts I discussed in earlier, on goals and your purpose, as well as using fear as a motivation.

Another great personal example of copying success relates to my experiences in learning languages. As I first mentioned in the Introduction, I started out my life thinking I was terrible at learning languages but someone urged me to seize the opportunity I was offered to go to the Monterey Defense Language Institute. I learned Russian, and a few years later I learned Japanese even better, to the point where I was thinking and dreaming in Japanese in about 18 to 20 months. What the instructors did was to teach me how to learn a language, first, by not accepting limits and perceptions of what I could or could not do. (After all, how hard could it be to learn Japanese or Russian when the dumbest person in those countries knows their native languages?) My success was certainly based on perseverance and a lot of hard work, but it was also the result of *following exactly what I was taught.* True, the supervisor in the first Russian class did occasionally threaten us, old Soviet-style, with the consequences of failing. But he also spent considerable time explaining how we first learned our own language and how we have to precisely duplicate that process in order to learn Russian.

In a broad sense, the process of copying something before improving it relates not only to exercise and language, but to virtually any endeavor, whether cooking, programming computers, designing buildings, or selling a product. If something is done much better than you can already do it, start by mimicking that process. Don't deviate. Why ad lib, when others have shown something works well? Then, when you've been able duplicate something with absolute precision and want to try an improvement, start by first changing only one part or step at a time.

Consider a recipe copied from a top chef, for example. It should be practiced until you can duplicate it exactly. Only at that point should you try to make a modification—but just one minor change at a time. If you made multiple modifications simultaneously and the recipe doesn't work out, it would be extremely difficult, if not impossible, to find out what specifically went wrong. Not only will you not know which ingredient was responsible for the failure, but you also won't be able to determine if the failure was caused by the interaction between particular ingredients that you changed or the interactions between one of your ingredients and any of the others. Should you have used 1.4 times ingredient X or 0.7 times ingredient Y? Statistically, there are actually an infinite number of possibilities.

Think this through: A top chef spends a huge amount of time testing and retesting a recipe before he or she is pleased with the final product. If you are copying a recipe from a well-respected chef, do you really think you are able to do better? Doesn't it seem a bit silly, as some might say, to just "Wing it"?
That said, I have one last side qualification: If you do get hold of one of the recipes of a "top" chef, they sometimes leave out something—a secret ingredient.

16

Peers, Friends and Family Can Be Harmful

'You are the average of the Five People You Spend the Most Time With"
~ Jim Rohn

It may sound peculiar, but when people wish you well, they really don't wish you *too* well. Let me explain.

While people generally like to see their families and friends succeed, there are other emotional factors in the back of their mind that undermine their good wishes. These factors include feelings of disbelief and jealousy, in addition to simple discomfort. If you become successful and do "too well," you may push into an area outside their comfort zone. Your friends may not only become uncomfortable with where you have moved in your life, but your role in *their* life; you may now be outside their circle of friends.

First, let's look at the issue of disbelief. Your friends and family members may not believe in your ability to successfully meet the challenge presented by the goal or task you've chosen. Why do they doubt you? Because those who have known you longest—maybe all your life—are the same people who have mental pictures of all the mistakes you've made or problems you've had in the past. They remember your past challenges and behavior–like when you were learning to ride a bicycle, or when you had trouble passing a test in college, or when you drank too much or did something else that may just be silly or stupid.

We've all heard how important first impressions are. Well, in this case where people have deep-rooted beliefs about you and your abilities, it is generally hard for them to imagine that you could attain something that seems far beyond the context in which they know you. That impression may be impossible to overcome; for some, it may be simply too much work to change their image of you. One thing you must realize is that your energy needs to be focused on your own progress, not on convincing anyone of the "new" you.

Additionally, your friends or family members may not believe that your goal or task itself is worthwhile. Or they may not see sufficient value in the expected result of your efforts. After all, this is not an initiative *they* would undertake. Not everyone wants to go to college or graduate school or learn a language or fight high-range forest fires.

Jealousy can also influence peoples' reaction to your potential success. In some cases, your success may mean their failure. In other cases, people will hold you back simply to prevent you from getting ahead or away from them, whatever the endeavor. Perhaps they are jealous because they've never tried to overcome a particular challenge, haven't seized the right opportunity to succeed, or haven't taken any action to change their situation. Think of what happens to couples, for example, when they divorce. When one ex-spouse gets remarried, it is common for the other unmarried person to be sad or jealous. Ultimately, the reason for their jealousy—whether it is disappointment in themselves or selfishness—doesn't matter.

In an earlier chapter, I introduced the concept of a person's comfort zone. When it comes to your success, the comfort zone of your peers, friends, and family becomes important because it overlaps yours. They are familiar with you and comfortable with the things you do. It's likely that you share similar interests and activities and are comfortable within relatively similar environments. But when your success begins to take you out of your comfort zone, you are probably stepping out of their comfort zone as well.

It is not your own comfort zone itself that affects you. Friends, families, and others have their own comfort zone of which you are a part. When you make a change, you introduce something unknown, unfamiliar, or uncomfortable to others—you've moved outside their comfort zone. The change might remind them of something they chose not to do or still wish they had done, or of their own weakness. Or they might feel uncomfortable because they are legitimately concerned that you are undertaking something unfamiliar, scary or dangerous, in their opinion, or just within their own discomfort. They may have the most altruistic of motivations, but the effect is the same. They will tend to discourage you in order to maintain their own comfort zone and where they see you fitting inside it. While you might be trying to make changes and progress in your life, your friends consciously or unconsciously will try to pull you back, whether out of true benevolence or jealousy.

Keep in mind that many people don't want to change or move from their current state or situation. They can't understand your desire to do what they resist. If you want to grow or achieve higher goals, you will meet resistance. I have heard it said that if you want to be in the top 1 percent of any endeavor, you will have to leave 99 percent behind. Sure, you may get together once in awhile, but most of your time will eventually be spent in other places.
To address this challenge, you will need to surround yourself with mentors and colleagues who have goals similar to yours and have already achieved success, or, like you, are in the process of growth. Some good examples of the importance of seeking friends and mentors come from the arena of sports.

Let's take a look, for instance, at what happens to people on the path to professional football. Star athletes in high school who perform well enough to play college football are an extremely small set of high school players. They are not only superstars in their school, but probably their league, county and state. In college, there will be relatively few who work hard enough and have the skill to be invited to the National Football League combine, where an even a smaller number of players compete in front of the NFL team scouts and recruiters. After that, a fraction of these players is drafted by a team and has the opportunity to go to training camp, where they compete to land a spot as a rookie on the team. (Even at this stage, many are brought into camp just to put pressure on the current players.) Near the end of training camp, every team, starting out at 90 players during training camp, will have to trim their roster to 53; 37 out of 90 will be sent home. Out of that final 53, there are probably minimally 45 that are already assured a place on the team based on prior performance on the team or another team. So, at most, 8 of the "extra" 50 invited will be kept as rookies. If these "rookies" work hard and competitively prove themselves, they may become regular NFL players. They are now an extremely select group that have proven themselves at several levels.

Now, let me pose a question: Do you think that players who make it to any professional team, whether male or female, are still practicing with their old high school friends? Of course not. They need to compete and learn from the best competitors and friends they can find, no matter how good a friend that high school buddy was. Female athletes, in fact, will sometimes practice with men or men's teams to raise their level competition or to hone their skills and advantages.

The same holds true for the field of academics. By the end of high school, students have competed to enter the college of their choice. Then, in college, they compete to get into the best graduate school, law school or medical school, based on their grades and other experiences. In the best graduate schools, students compete against the best of the best. Now you can see why I previously noted that it's best to figure out not what you need to know, but rather what you don't know. Just moving ahead of the average of your achieving high school friends will not bring you near excellence. You are ultimately competing against yourself, not your current group of friends or colleagues.

It's unfortunate that the students who did the best in school, often are not necessarily the ones with the greatest potential. Many others dropped out or were dissuaded from success by some of the people around them, including family, friends, even teachers. At every level of success in life, there will be people who don't necessarily want you to succeed. Many just don't want you to leave their world.

Think of the ways people around you hold you back. It doesn't matter whether their methods involve disbelief, sarcasm, or teasing—they all suck energy from you. Your efforts to confront them are both unnecessary and futile, as you will not change them. Instead, look for positive forces to aid your own development. That means you must constantly search for people with similar interests, or mentors or coaches who have already attained what you are seeking— usually outside your current group of contacts. For example, let's say you want to expand your skills in photography or video because you want to improve your social media marketing. You might join a group or a Meetup of people in your area, which could offer an opportunity to meet and expand your friendships into areas outside your comfort zone. Push yourself to new levels and become deaf to your current friends and "audience." Yes, those around you are like an audience. We often act with the hope or expectation of approval from those around us. If you are serious about growth or change, you need a new audience for acceptance and approval.

One interesting way for students to find new "audiences" today is to seek out internship programs. I know that internships are frequently unpaid, and interns often receive little or no stipend for their room and board. To some students, this appears a lot like slave labor. But others see it as an opportunity to get to know a company, build a résumé, and to make contacts for the future. While some companies that are using internships to take advantage of unpaid help, this still may be a way for students to develop future contacts, find new audiences—and push themselves outside their comfort zone. If you are older, "going back to school" may be no more than an organization where you learn about a new skill or endeavor, or a Mastermind where you get the support and protection of a learning environment.

I have no problem with people who consciously decide to drop out of school at any level to do something that gives current gratification and deliberately does not use their potential. Let me re-emphasize my view as an economist: When I see someone choose something that most other people may feel is not as beneficial to their longer term future, that is known as individual choice. I do have a problem, however, with those who whine, complain about or are jealous of others who push forward and advance themselves. Individual choice reflects the preference of the individual, and the pursuit of satisfaction or income in the present, at the expense of the future, is part of conscious choice. I can't say that either investing your time and effort for the future or reaping current satisfaction is right or wrong. I can say that it is a choice and you can't have both. The statistic that 80% of the wealthy in the U.S. today started from poverty is a shocking statistic. But what did that 80% give up, and how much did they push themselves to attain their level of success?

For children and adults alike, one of the most important life lessons to learn—and teach others—is to avoid peer pressure. This kind of harmful influence is a major problem that prevents so many people from advancing. I'm talking about not only the pressure to take drugs or follow the latest dangerous trend or fad, but also the pressure that comes from expressions used in school or at work to limit your efforts. For example, how many times have you heard comments such as, "You've done enough and should take a break and have some fun?" This is peer pressure, and you must decide whether to spend your time investing in your future or pursuing a current pleasure. I cannot say which is the right decision for you, but the decisions you make at such moments throughout your life determine where you will end up later. Time is one commodity that you can neither save nor store. When each day is over, all time—86,400 seconds—are spent. The next day, you start on a new day. But how you spend your time is a choice. Everyone gets the same 86,400 seconds per day. How will you use them? For today, did you invest your time investing in your future or squander it all on frills, mind-numbing games or mindless TV or conversations whose purpose you can't even remember?

Peer pressure can be one of the most negative forces you will need to overcome. I have successfully mentored a couple of college students in ways to thwart peer pressure. I stressed two points. First, the students needed to realize that most if not all of these people who seemed so dear to them were probably not even going to be in their life in three years. (Remember the football analogy.) In college they will probably have different interests and majors. After college they will all go in different directions. Three years after graduation they will probably not be in contact with the peers they had in college.

The second point is that, in order not to be ostracized, students needed a way to alleviate the pressure put on them. If they truly wanted to succeed, they had to postpone some enjoyments and invest in their future by working in the present. Their future lay in their own hands, so they shouldn't allow their peers to interfere with their college studies. Because that is easier said than done, they needed methods with which to thwart the pressure. As mentioned previously, one approach was to find a place hidden away in the library where a student could quietly study. Then, when somebody or a group insisted that the student join them for dinner, or accompany them to a party or out for coffee, the student could say, "Great, but I have to do something first. As soon as I'm done, I'll meet you there." Yes, I used this often while at college.

Pressure and criticism from anyone can be overwhelming, even devastating, for anyone. You must find ways to combat that pressure, not by arguing with others, but by eliminating its effect on you. When you stop making progress to satisfy current desires, your future success will be affected—and usually not in a good way. There are exceptions, but relatively few. You may win the lottery, but if that is your plan, you have no plan.

17

Program your Mind through Visualization

'I train myself mentally with visualization. The morning of a tournament, before I put my feet on the floor, I visualize myself making perfect runs with emphasis on technique, all the way through to what my personal best is in practice.... The more you work with this type of visualization, ... you'll actually begin to feel your muscles contracting at the appropriate times.'
-Camille Duvall – Five Time World Champion Water Skier

To perform most of its daily chores, the human body uses involuntary actions without regard to reasoning or thinking—these are known as reflex actions, like breathing, walking, and blinking to keep the eyes moist. Similarly, when we perform a certain task so often that we no longer have to think about it, it essentially becomes a reflex action. Look at athletes—boxers, football, tennis and baseball players, for example—who work on the fundamentals of their sport to the point that their training makes many of their actions an automatic response—a reflex action. When you are advancing in any skill your brain knows what to do by what you have already experienced; now it has more resources to use and coordinate with those new tasks you are attempting.

Think of visualization in the same way: not so much as a mental technique as a "programming of the mind." It works in much the same way as when someone works hard and certain things become reflex actions, blending the imagination and the incredible power of the brain to help facilitate success in dreams and goals.

Imagine all the things that go through the brain whenever we do anything. It seems only reasonable to reduce the unpredictability by training it with new actions and reflexes so the brain can work its magic. Additionally, the more your brain is at least familiar with the task at hand, the greater the confidence you will develop.

The brain has enormous power, much of it rarely used. We may all have experienced times where we are telling ourselves that we can't do something or at least have doubts about our ability. By visualizing successfully doing or completing something, we are in effect getting the brain to help us figure out a successful outcome rather than accepting failure or uncertainty.

It works in everything from school tests to sports, even giving speeches and dating. (The last one I'll leave for you to figure out!) Used properly, visualization can improve our life, our performance and the speed at which we achieve certain goals. From the opposite vantage point, you may have heard the expression, "If you can't see it, you can't do it." Well, with visualization, we are seeing the outcome in the best possible light and within our mind as we see and work through many of the obstacles in our path.

Let's look at some of the many excellent examples from sports. If you watched the 2010 Winter Olympics, you would have seen the great alpine skier Lindsey Vonn at the starting gate moving her head and arms as she visualized every turn and bump on the hill before she left the starting gate just before her gold medal run. I used this kind of visualization to help my own skiing. I found a few YouTube videos demonstrating some of the skiing techniques I needed to reach the next level and watched a couple of them several times right before skiing. As I drove up to the ski resort each time, I imagined myself following the same patterns that were on this videos. Every time I did this, I was building the movements into my memory and found it easier to accelerate my progress. My brain had already experienced the moguls and steep runs even though I had yet to arrive at the slopes. My success became evident.

Baseball offers another good example of the opportunity to use visualization. When in a slump, some professional players will go back to videos of themselves batting when they were on a hot streak. This helps the players picture themselves in the same stance and swing as when they were doing well their mind; their minds see what actions they were doing when they were hitting .300, not .210. Remember, the brain gives instructions to the rest of the body and tells it how and when to move. Every muscle, big and small, gets the appropriate instructions from the brain, so by visualization, you are actually helping the brain re-create the correct actions.

The benefit of visualization was also demonstrated by an Australian psychologist, Alan Richardson, who tested basketball players' ability to shoot free throws. He divided them into three groups. The first group practiced 20 minutes per day. The second group would only visualize the free throws and did not practice. The third group neither practiced nor did any visualization. They were the control group. The second group had significant improvement and was almost as improved as the first group that practiced.

Sometimes you will hear a person say they prefer to sit back and think about their performance or just go practice. But they actually may be limiting the brain's ability. They are focusing on the conscious mind and not all those things the brain does without thinking through an action. In general, it should take a lot longer as they work it out and restudy what they are doing. In many cases, they may exacerbate the problems they are having. Why? When they are thinking through the problem, the most recent behavior and events will be foremost in the mind. So if they are a baseball player, for example, whatever took them off good and proper form or technique will not necessarily be something they will eliminate by thinking through it. After all, whatever thoughts they had were probably what put them in a slump in the first place.

In bodybuilding or weightlifting, visualization is also critical—as I learned not only from observing others, but my own first-hand experience. I mentioned in an earlier chapter, many years ago my friend Joe taught me weightlifting to help improve my strength. Besides increasing my strength Joe taught me a lot about setting goals, copying well—and visualizing an exercise before I started it. Several years later, when I was lifting much heavier weights on my own, I found myself a couple times in a rush starting to exercise. I could not even get the weight off the ground. I quickly realized my mistake; I forgot the importance of visualizing. I thought to myself, "Better step back, relax and visualize the lift." At that point, I approached the weights, pictured myself doing the exercise, put my hands in the proper position and easily did my three complete sets of 8 to 12 repetitions. If you ever see weightlifting competitions on TV, you can see participants doing the same kind of visualizing before doing their lifts.

Visualization is not only important in sports, but in virtually everything from giving speeches to taking tests. If you are about to give a speech, particularly if it's in a unfamiliar environment, you should arrive a bit early to look over the room and picture yourself giving the speech. It will be a very different speech, depending upon whether the room is large or small, how it is laid out and whether it's dark or well-lit. When I first heard this idea, it did sound a little silly. But I heard it from a reliable, experienced speaker, and remembering the lesson of learning by copying the masters, I followed his advice, exactly. And I learned that this experience of viewing yourself in the room beforehand allows your brain to be comfortable with the situation so that when the time comes, your mind will be concentrating on fewer items—that is, there will be fewer variables for the brain to calculate. Many of your questions about the environment will already be addressed.

The same applies to taking an exam someplace that is unfamiliar. You may realize the need to find a seat in a particular place away from some heat or air conditioning or in front of the room, away from other distractions. Just seeing the room itself will make the situation feel a little more familiar. This is one of the first and most important points of visualization. You are reducing unknown variables, such as parts of the environment, in order to concentrate on the task at hand.

So there are at least two important aspects to visualization. First, you are allowing the brain to become familiar with parts of the task that you are going to undertake. It doesn't matter if it's for speech in a larger auditorium or on the ski slope. You are also allowing the brain to start solving some of the problems needed to complete the task, including the involuntary muscle actions that are necessary for completion.

Second, visualization reduces tension and helps you maintain a calm presence and start to build confidence. After you visualize exactly what you want your body to do, you've actually pictured yourself successfully completing what you are about to do. With the success already in the mind, you maintain a calmer presence and increase the ability to do well. Like athletes, professional dancers also use this practice to attain faster movements or lift their legs higher. And Emilie Autumn, a great violinist, has stated that her music skills were developed largely by mentally playing a particular piece of music at night.

While visualization seems easy to apply to sports or public performances, it may be harder to imagine applying it to an area like studying. But if you imagine yourself having a hard time studying or feel you are not good at something, guess what? *You're not going to be good at it.* In much harder tasks or projects, you have to look at improvement in small steps. You may need to visualize yourself completing a test on time or studying in your room. You need to develop the positive mental images through visualization. To be a good student, it's important to develop confidence in yourself and your studying by slowly believing that you actually like learning.

This is true for any type of learning, whether you're a young student or an older adult. And if you think about it, it's essential to keep learning, because when you stop learning in life, what has your life become? Even if you're no longer trying to learn math or a language when you're older you may want to learn to be better as a photographer or a gardener.

Inevitably, when you enter this new arena, there will be a period of discomfort that needs to be overcome—and visualization can help you do it.

I thought about this point recently when I was on an airport shuttle bus going to the Seattle terminal. Sitting near me was a family returning to Minnesota—a nice couple with a cute 2-year-old. But next to them was a woman, probably in her 60's, who started to paint a horrible picture in the little girl's mind about how long and what an ordeal the plane ride would be. The girl looked concerned and extremely uncomfortable. I quickly took over the conversation and repainted a picture of how nice the ride would be and how the girl would see neat stuff. The mother joined me. It was great to see the change in the girl's outlook as she started to imagine this nice flight. She visualized a good time and experience—the way it surely would be.

In short, the lesson I have tried to share with you is this: Visualization is not some magic show trick, but rather something that you consciously do to assist the brain in what it is about to do.

18

Don't Allow 'Can't' Into Your Vocabulary

The single most powerful element of youth is our inability to know what's impossible.
~Adam Braun – Author, Founder of Pencils of Promise

One of the most debilitating words in the English language is "can't." Think about this for a moment: As soon as a person or company says they can't do something they have, in effect, quit. And yet, every invention or innovation in the world was achieved by somebody who solved a problem when somebody else said it couldn't be done. This does not mean you can solve every problem in the world. However, when you take the attitude that it is no longer possible to solve it, you certainly won't.

Removing negative attitudes and refocusing your thoughts can be easier than you think. Saying "can't" goes far beyond the projection of attitude that you hear from motivational speakers. If you fully understand the concept of not using "can't" in this chapter, I promise you will see leaps in your ability to succeed.

Problem-solving is one of the most important skills in life. There are normally two components to this skill. The first is the effect of a person's attitude on their drive to seek a solution to any problem. The second is an approach used to reach a goal that breaks a problem into two pieces, known versus unknown. It employs an almost mathematical method, but anyone can do this; it really doesn't require any advance understanding of mathematics.
Attitude is well covered and discussed in so many books and articles that I won't spend much time on it. Everything you need to know about attitude can be summarized in the amazing story of Jennifer Bricker, the gymnast born without legs, whom I mentioned in Chapter 10. Abandoned at birth by her parents in Romania, she was adopted by an American family in a remote Illinois town with a population of about 50 people. Her adoptive parents, Gerald and Sharon Bricker, were determined to raise her from an early age

just like her three able-bodied brothers—never to accept the word "can't."

And she didn't. She pursued her greatest love, gymnastics, not to mention volleyball, softball, even basketball. She became the first athlete with physical disabilities to become tumbling champion in Illinois—competing against able-bodied athletes. Later, she discovered, incredibly, that she was actually the biological sister of her childhood idol, Olympic gold-medal-winning gymnast Dominique Moceanu.

Today, Jennifer works as a professional acrobat and aerialist, touring with celebrities like Britney Spears. Jennifer Bricker does not believe in the word "can't"—and neither should you. There is a saying I've have heard many times: "Whether you say you can or you can't, you are correct." It seems a little simplistic, but does bring home the point—the effect either a positive or negative attitude has on success.

Now let's turn to a very different and somewhat harder concept that requires more explanation, but if you use it well, you can actually achieve better results and greater success. This concept involves using "cannot" as a limiting factor in process of seeking a solution. I like to use mathematical problems as an analogy for using this approach to increase the speed and probability of successful problem-solving, in work or life. When solving math problems, you usually have a set of assumptions. Those assumptions can be thought of as conditions or aspects for which you do not have a solution As soon as you say can't solve the problem, what will happen? You won't solve it. Instead, let's imagine that you were able to get it partially solved. At that point, you still have some unanswered questions, but you've also made progress in solving the problem. Depending on the level of somebody's confidence in solving problems, some will stop here and say they can't complete it.

In business, this is usually an unacceptable position. At one company I owned, I refused to allow anyone to use the terms "can't" or "cannot"—to the frustration to most of my employees. Frequently, someone would come to me and say, "I know you don't want to hear this, but..." and then would proceed to tell me that something couldn't be done. The problem with this type of behavior is that the person was telling me that they wanted to give up. Each time, I would painstakingly explain that it was important to figure out as much as they could, rather than declaring they couldn't fully solve the problem. They've eliminated parts of the problem, so the problem was reduced. Now, input from somebody else could bring us further toward a solution.

Even in a situation where we might not know the final "answer," by solving as much as possible, we were able to make much better estimates and better understand the potential effects of our recommendations. If the CEO of a major company is making a decision, that decision must ultimately be made, and by solving parts of the problem and reducing the unknown, isn't the probability of a better decision increased? In the real world of business, decisions often need to be made without complete answers, but by narrowing the problem the decisions could be optimal.

You could apply such an approach to simple problems, such as planning a trip. While one person might quickly conclude that he can't make a trip because he doesn't have enough money, another focuses on the unsolved issue of how he can get enough money. Perhaps he could get to his destination by alternative transportation, or if traveling by car, investigate whether he could invite someone to share the expense. While this case might seem trivial, we have all seen many people quickly stop considering a plan or quit a project with similar speed. I have friends living upstate New York, for example, who wanted to go to a conference in Dallas. They went together in one car, split the expense of the hotel and were able to go. Many complex problems often have similar simple solutions. In solving problems, you will always run across obstacles. It is up to you as to how or when you might overcome these obstacles.

Sometimes the solution is so obvious that you wonder why nobody stopped to think of it. One problem for decades, if not centuries, was carrying luggage. When we look at luggage today with wheels on it, it seems silly that it didn't exist until sometime in the 1990s. I hope someone made a fortune with the idea of putting wheels on luggage or on coolers, which is so obvious in hindsight. I remember how we used to get two guys to each grab a handle to lug a cooler to a picnic bench. We should never accept the status quo as something that doesn't have a better solution.

However, given what we knew at the time, success was two strong guys carrying a cooler.

Let's consider a much bigger example of problem-solving: the production of an electric car by General Motors. In 1980 I had the opportunity to test drive an early iteration of the electric car, when there were lots of reasons people could have concluded, "It can't be done." It was a monumental project, with many obstacles to overcome. The batteries took up a tremendous amount of space and were very heavy. The cost of replacing these batteries were also prohibitive. And there were environmental concerns, charging station availability, potential fire hazards, and vehicle performance.

But General Motors did not conclude that the electric car could not be built. GM's electric car, the Volt, was finally released in late 2010. Even today, it has some significant problems: Its cost of production is still too high; it depends too heavily on government subsidies; its range between charges is too modest; and there will always be a problem recycling the batteries. However, it is getting much closer to becoming a widely available consumer product.

GM still has problems to solve. As I wrote this, it appeared that the company was planning to change the Volt from a Chevrolet to a Cadillac, so it could charge more. Of course, that wouldn't fix the cost problem, but would move the car to a much higher income customer. Currently, that may actually be a wise decision. The higher-earning Cadillac buyer is less deterred by some of the cost factors and may be willing to pay more for the environmental claims.

The difference between stating that you can't solve a problem, versus stating that you still have part of the problem to solve is more than subtle. It often is the difference between success and failure. As soon as you say you can't, then you are done, finished. But if you state that you still have parts to complete or some questions to answer, your mind will continue to search for answers. The difference is more than just the difference between an optimist and a pessimist. Hopefully, you ask others for help and build on the problems they've already solved. That's exactly what some of the Japanese car manufacturers did, learning from the problems General Motors solved, then solving some more themselves, thereby building a more marketable electric car. This is not to take anything from the Japanese manufacturers. This is the smart thing to do. Take existing technology, improve it and solve new problems.

I do understand that the word "can't" may be used by many people to de-stress their job or personal life. That is, they use it to defuse a problem so that it is no longer something they should be expected to do. If I say, "I can't," then it can't be expected of me. It is no longer a problem. Unfortunately, that decision also limits or throttles your ability to succeed. Think back to the earlier chapter on comfort zones, and learning to love being uncomfortable in order to make progress. Instead of fearing what you don't know, embrace the concept. It means you are growing, expanding your comfort zone and solving problems.

The other side of can't is "just doing" it before you know what "it" is. In other words, make sure you know what the breadth and scope of the problem is that you are attempting to solve. What I find particularly interesting is the number of decisions people make when they are not even close to understanding what the problem is. Whether in business or in our personal life, we often need to make some of the biggest choices or decisions before we can comprehend the problem's full scope.

It doesn't matter whether we're deciding which major to choose in college, which house to buy, which camera to buy or whether our company should buy another company or go forward on a new product. Of course, we rarely have all the information to make the perfect decision. And yes, in every case a decision needs to be made. To increase the odds of a great outcome, we need to know the problem and not ignore any piece of the decision. Those items that we don't know yet might be answered by someone else or researched, rather than grabbing the easy escape by saying "I can't" or "I don't know."

In choosing a college major, a student may start by at least eliminating things they don't want to do and find uninteresting. I might also suggest that they leave out those areas that lead nowhere. They may be great for hobbies in the future, but what is your purpose now? Hopefully, they also will eliminate careers where they have little chance finding employment after college.

Another seemingly simple example is choosing a camera. Many people just buy what they will use now and move up over time. Then they have a string of cameras that are really a waste of money. So it is better to think of it as a problem we need to solve. We need to determine how much or whether some of the capabilities of various cameras are useful to us. Unless we are professionals, we need to learn what some capabilities really mean—and whether we will ever learn or bother to use those features. Finally, of course, do we want to spend the extra money on some additional features? This becomes more difficult when we don't know what those features, how difficult they are to implement or whether we will ever learn how to use them. Even after we learn these features, will we want to use the camera, or is it really just too much trouble for the type of pictures we will take?

Choosing a major or a camera seems quite simple, compared to making a decision to go forward with a major corporate or career decision. But in all cases, the way to increase your probability of success is to reduce uncertainty, eliminating what you don't know. If you have to make a decision where you must guess or estimate, it will become a far more accurate estimate when you narrow the focus.

In short, we are approaching the decision-making process in this mathematical way, by increasing information and eliminating parts of the problem or at least increasing our knowledge about the problem. Ultimately, this does lead to a more informed estimate or decision. After all, if business is to succeed it has to move forward with the best information possible. More important, if your life is to succeed, you need to make the best decisions possible, and the more we limit the guesswork, the more we increase the probability of a better plan or solution. Remember, making wrong decisions, as well as not making any decision, wastes time that you never can get back.

And time is an important factor in all life decisions. Be wary of procrastination (discussed in Chapter 14), which leads to delays and indecision that block the path to success. There is usually a time limit to success, and it is usually best realized that your life, career and education all are more appealing if you haven't overstayed your welcome in any position in your career or education.

Chapter 19

Turn Jealousy into a Learning Opportunity

'Resentment is like drinking poison and
waiting for the other person to die'
— Carrie Fisher

Pretty much everyone knows that jealousy is a negative emotion. It can be doubly damaging, too, because it goes in two directions: Jealousy can be expressed by you when you're jealous of others, or it can come from another person who is jealous of you. Either way, jealousy can be debilitating. It is not always easy to eliminate, and sometimes not even easy to recognize.

How do you prevent yourself from becoming jealous or avoid being affected by the jealousy of others?

First, let's look at the broad impact of jealousy, whether you are the initiator or the recipient of such feelings. Jealousy adversely affects both mental and physical states of the body. It can affect your personality and emotional state—making you angry and aggressive—and alter beliefs in yourself, even the health of your digestive system. Jealousy invites unfavorable judgment by others and a negative perception of your maturity level. And it can rob you of any opportunity for any positive development or action.

Generally, as the level of jealousy increases, the prospect for success decreases. The emotional energy used when people are jealous limits the ability of anyone to succeed. It doesn't matter if jealousy is directed from you toward others, or from others toward you. Jealousy limits people's ability to better themselves by not allowing them to focus on their goals. Feelings of jealousy often increase; the more important a person is in your life. These negative feelings impose on your thoughts and affect your performance; you're spending time being jealous when you should be thinking about what's needed for change and progress.

Jealousy, then, becomes an ego-substitute for performance. Rather than focus on what you need to do or learn to become successful, you're rationalizing your own lack of performance in the face of others' success.

Sometimes jealousy becomes a mental safety mechanism--it's much easier to be jealous of someone else than find solutions to your own issues or problems. How many times have you heard something like, "He makes me so jealous?" Doesn't that seem silly? You become jealous; nobody *makes* you jealous. Jealousy easily translates into an excuse for why others gets desirable things in life and you don't. First rule: Life is not fair. There are a lot of random things that happen over the course of a lifetime and everyone gets their share of good and bad. Some focus more on the good and building from what they receive, while others dwell and waste time and energy on the bad. Guess who wins? So when you hear the expression, "Life's not fair," the appropriate response is: "Get over it."

Jealousy also implies competition or some comparison you're making between yourself and someone else. But remember our discussion from previous chapters: If you truly want to succeed, you need to focus on competing with *yourself*. Learn from others, but fill in your own holes of skills or knowledge. You know what you need to do. Compete against your own successes and knowledge. Focus on what you don't know, not what the other person knows--unless your specific goal is to learn from them.

Why should you be even comparing yourself to others at all, except to learn and understand how something was done? That is, if they can do it, you can do it--just learn or improve upon it. I do realize, of course, that there are limitations here. I'm not referring to a 5' 2" guy, for example, thinking he could play nose tackle in the National Football League. That's delusional. If someone is jealous of someone else's accomplishments, they need to learn from it rather than waste time and energy on whining. Furthermore, a jealous person emits negative emotions that make them uncomfortable to be around, and therefore they rarely receive the help and reassurance they need from others. If a person did receive compassion when they appeared jealous, that would simply reinforce their negative feelings. If a jealous person were having a difficult time or experience, they might need someone to just listen, but just chiming in with sympathy might not help. It could even aggravate the negative effects of jealousy interfering with real problem-solving, and perhaps making a change to more positive behavior increasingly difficult.

So, how does someone turn negative jealous emotions in a positive direction?

To convert jealousy to a positive force, you need to go through three quick stages: Recognize it; reposition your view of it; then turn it into a positive.
If, for example, someone benefits from a lucky coincidence such as a lottery, it would be easy to say, "Gee that could have (or *should* have!) been me." But holding onto that jealous emotion does absolutely no good. Quite frankly it's ridiculous, but it often occurs. We need to get rid of it, quickly, by changing our perception of such incidents. That is, if something is truly random luck, such as the lottery, there is no reason for jealousy. It's just silly to focus your attention on the chance of being the 1-in-200 million, more or less, winner in the lottery of life. (Actually, if you play that sort of lottery on a regular basis, you probably should re-read this book from the beginning and re-focus on a real life!)

On the other hand, if your jealousy results from desiring something someone else *earned*, ask yourself: Why should I be jealous of something that can be admired or even supported? In a supportive role, you have the opportunity to both learn from someone who has earned success—instead of feeling jealous toward them. If you can truly feel good for that person, he or she may even share what they did. Positive emotions will bring far more assistance than negative ones. What skills did the person have? Were they always looking for opportunities, networking, making themselves valuable to others? How many times have you heard the expression, "They were just in the right place at the right time?" Well, there are usually a multitude of reasons that account for someone being "in the right place at the right time." Also, there are reasons these people appear to be "chosen" for success. Don't bother with the trivial reasons, the advantages people may have gotten through their family connections, for example, that you can't attain. Instead, look at every opportunity someone else gets as an opportunity for you to learn. If you maintain this outlook, you will also increase your network and friendships, too.

Now, what should you do if you are the recipient of another person's jealousy? This person could range from a competitor who considers you almost as an enemy, to a friend who perceives that you have taken an opportunity away from them. Think of all the people who think the world is like a pie. If you take a piece of the pie, they feel that there is less for them. That may be true for a pie, but in real life, they are ignoring trends like broad economic growth or the collective increase in human knowledge. (You, too, may feel guilty or responsible if you're susceptible to those thoughts.)

A friend who is jealous of you is not a true friend—certainly not someone whose opinion you should consider. Jealousy may even extend to family members. You may still love them as family, but realize where their input is in your life. Don't risk other relationships for the sake of protecting theirs or comforting them. Recalling the chapter on friends and family, it may be time for you to spend less time with a jealous person, even if they are a member of your family. While many people are concerned with improving and increasing the goods they have (cars, houses, clothes,) they shouldn't forget to constantly improve their network of friends. Interesting, the desire to have things that are better than someone else often leads to comparisons of others and keeps a person from developing new friendships that may be better than the ones causing them problems.

Jealousy is highly related to a false ego, rigidness of opinion and superficial relationships. Jealousy impedes any happiness; it will reap possessiveness instead of gratitude for what you have. It will foster insecurity rather than confidence. You may even feel shame for not doing something instead of just doing it.

Don't get me wrong here; I'm not saying that you should isolate yourself from others. I try to relate to everyone who crosses my path in life. I get along very well with my garbage collector, my mailman, the counter person at a coffee shop or front desk clerk at a hotel. When I lived in San Francisco, I really learned a lot from an elderly man next door. While he was poor, black and an alcoholic most of his life, he was very attentive to personal relationships, especially the kids around him. He was pensive, wise; he harbored no jealousy. As I often say, you truly can learn something from just about everyone.

Yes, someone else will win the lottery or possibly get some better breaks. But if you keep working, learning new things on your own and from others-- instead of coveting their successes—your breaks, too, will likely increase. That certainly has been the case for me.

Opportunities do come to those who project a positive attitude that attracts other successful people into their life. If you turn jealousy into a learning opportunity, you will come across more positively. You will make more opportunities for yourself and will start recognizing when your opportunity arrives. People are more likely to want to be around you—and after a while, you might find that you like yourself more, too. All of these set you up for more successes.

20

Whatever Happened to Sacrifice?

'Live for Today, you might die tomorrow! -
What if I Live!'
~ Thomas O'Grady, PhD

What exactly do we mean when we say, "It takes sacrifice to be successful"? What kind of sacrifice does it take, and what does that mean for me?

I'm sure you've seen all the stories and ads about how to become an overnight success in 30 days or 90 days. I get emails almost every day proclaiming that if you follow the sender's system you'll start making either five figures per month or seven figures per year. Hearing the hype on robo-calls, at sales conferences and TV channels everywhere, you continually are hit with get-rich schemes or scams. They certainly make it seem like there short cuts to success, and they always have someone to give a testimonial, serving as an example or witness to a success story. These are tempting sales pitches, but even if they do offer more efficient ways to become successful, "miracles" should not be given as promises.

I do know one person who appears to have become extremely successful fairly quickly. She has a unique product and close connections to the manufacturers of her product. She was also one of the first people in her industry to exploit online sales around the world. Those are a lot of unique conditions. Now, there are two other people I know—there may be more—who claim on their web site that they've had the same success she's had. Even if a person had all of her advantages, who do you believe? Some things just don't add up.

Well, fortunately for me, when I was young I didn't fall for those get-rich-quick promotions and ended up taking a much more lucrative path—through sacrifice. Since I am good at remembering numbers and asking questions, always drilling down for further understanding, I realized that those proclamations of six or seven figures were truly unrealistic. Take a good look at income distribution statistics for our society: The promise of overnight success sounds great, but let's not dwell on the one or two people who seem to have a magical success story and concentrate on ensuring those successes that can be achieved with much higher probability. (By the way, some of those folks who claim such high revenue are simply not telling the truth. Many others are not telling you that their expenses are almost as high as revenue—and they can't even buy a home or pay cash for their car!)

Many testimonials on TV or on billboard ads will tout how people got rich playing the lottery or betting at the race track or in Las Vegas. Does that mean these places are good "investments" for your time or money? Of course not. Over the years, I've gotten tired of hearing people tell me they "always win" when they go to Vegas or Atlantic City. Really? I started saying to these people, "Isn't it remarkable how benevolent these casino owners are? They build these massive, beautiful buildings and yet, they give away so much money." When they asked me, "What do you mean?' I replied that everyone I knew told me they were winners, so the casinos must be giving money away. The proclamations stopped.

So instead of counting on wishes, promises and false expectations, are you willing to put in the work and sacrifice for your future? Let's discuss how you can truly be successful through sacrifice. The easiest way of explaining this is to draw a parallel to saving.

When you invest for your retirement, the earlier you start saving, the easier it is to achieve your long-term goals. Whether you are 30, 40, 50 or older, if you do live past 90 (which may well be in the cards, since according to the Social Security Administration, most of us will live past 85), what are your plans for an inspiring and fulfilled life? At some point, your ability to work will end, and when that happens you will need savings to carry you to the end.

In a 2011 Harris Poll, 61% of people surveyed said they are afraid of outliving their retirement savings. The question is, will you have made enough sacrifices earlier in life to accumulate such savings? It is important to put aside a bit of money over time for your future. It is even better if you have a lump sum to start as the initial investment or put aside some unexpected income.

You can look at your career in a similar fashion, starting out with a "lump sum" in the form of education and training. And there are plenty of careers that are available later on in life if you are willing to sacrifice some free time—including your TV or "hanging out" time."

My own investment in the future followed this concept of establishing a small lump sum and creating ongoing savings for 40+ years. I know, many people have commented on how lucky I was to get the breaks I had. But outside my chance meeting with two guys on the train during my basic training years—an incident I mentioned earlier—you know by now that my road to success was far from luck. If you are continually working toward goals, you will constantly learn new things. As you learn new skills, you also open up new ideas and opportunities. You are making your own luck.

Let me go back to a story I first related in Chapter 3, "Are You Able?" When I was younger, I was always told that the key to success was to go to college and then, when you wanted to develop a higher-end career, you had to go to either law school, graduate school, medical school or business school. So I had to sit down and figure out how to do that. (Remember, at the time I didn't think I was very bright.)

Even while serving in the military and before entering college, I realized I needed to make sacrifices in order to position myself as the best student possible when applying for graduate schools. Here was my logic. I had figured out that when I returned to college I would have three years left to complete college. I knew that when you apply to graduate school, decisions by schools are made during the last semester. In my case, that meant that I would have 2½ years of grades to be evaluated. So if I considered the 2½ years as an investment in the rest of my life, it would be like a 2½-year push toward a retirement fund. However, the big difference is that the graduate school I entered would be the continuing ticket for entry into careers for 50 to 60 or more years. In the same way, this approach can relate to almost anything you want to do: Building good skills or training should be your ticket to opportunities in your future.

My next step was to evaluate how I could get great grades and what might hinder me from doing so. I realized that when I went back into college there would be some courses that would be easier for me and others that would not. Yet, in order to get into the best possible graduate program for whatever I chose, I had to have great grades overall. I needed to reduce my weaknesses and complete any courses while in the military that I might find particularly difficult later on. (Remember Chapter 5, "Know your Weaknesses and Go on a Diet.") So I used my remaining time in the military to prepare for my college career.

Additionally, I understood that if I was going to dedicate myself to my studies upon my return to college, I would not be able to take outside jobs. While still in the military, then, I had to take outside work to save money so I wouldn't have to work while attending school. I knew that meant that I might be working or attending a class at the same time my army peers were out partying. By almost anybody's standards, these choices would be considered sacrifices. After all, everyone else was "having fun." But sometimes you have to refocus your decision to find it attractive. In my case, I had dreams and plans.

I decided that if I was to be successful—as I defined success—I would have to work much harder than most other people. I wanted to get great grades, even though I believed I was not even an average student. In setting aside 2½ years of college to attain my goals, I also knew that I would have to put my social life on hold. Sacrifice was part of the plan.

My peers in the military (and I should say almost everyone around us) spent their nights out drinking and then, at work the next day, talking about what went on the previous night. Quite frankly, I couldn't understand their enthusiasm. They were just rehashing the previous night, laughing a lot at themselves and each other about all the silly things they did together. Meanwhile, I just sat off to the side, doing work when needed—but with lots of free time, I also studied to prepare for college. Yes, that was a sacrifice: I took a different path, but I was investing my free time. I knew where I was going and had a plan how to get there.

Part of what I felt was probably what you, too, have experienced in your life: negative peer pressure. I talked about this issue in Chapter 16 ("Beware of Friends and Family") about how those close to you can slow you down or actually try to stop your progress. You must find ways to resist temptations and fight or ignore peer pressure, especially when you recognize the need for personal sacrifice.

This kind of pressure on you *not* to invest in your future happens on a regular basis. How many times have you heard a friend say, "Oh come on, you've worked enough, you deserve a break"? One time, when a bunch of military friends were together in my room, one of them asked me why I was saving so much money for college. He said, "Just think about it, you might die tomorrow." My immediate response was "True, but what if I live?"

Now, much later in life—even in your 50s or older—you can change your career within a few years. It does take some sacrifice. If you want to be among the best in your chosen field, you need to invest your time and energy at the beginning to gain entry into the best opportunities. I'm not going to say that there are any guarantees of success nor that what you choose will be the best for you. I, personally, have had a couple of businesses over the years that I dumped because laws changed, thus altering the economics of the industry and making them undesirable. But with an attitude of sacrifice for the future and dedication and perseverance, I was able to shake off disappointments and jump into the next opportunity.

Finally, remember this: Sacrifice for a short period of time is truly a small investment over the long term. Investing in your future, when treated properly, is similar to the concept of compound interest. Just as compounding interest can make your wealth multiply faster, a good investment into your career, business or skills can lead to an abundance of new friends, new opportunities, and multiple successes!

Still, it will not be easy. There are many crossroads in people's lives and sacrifice is usually the harder path. You need to use the tactics and ideas you learned earlier in this book to motivate yourself past the temptation of the easiest paths. Just as you would sacrifice buying that shiny new electronic gadget for the opportunity to put a little more money into your retirement savings, you must make choices and assess what is necessary for you to have a comfortable life long into the future.

If you choose not to sacrifice, that is a legitimate choice open to you. It is, however, a conscious decision to do something now—and potentially miss out on a better future. What is *not* legitimate is to be jealous of those that did sacrifice and ended up having what you might have had if you followed the more difficult path.

Ultimately, most success is something that you feel you overcame or worked or saved hard to reach. It is like winning in a sport. The main difference is that this kind of success can truly stay with you and shape you for more and bigger successes. Repeated successes build your confidence in everything you do. Do not forget this lesson as you labor through sacrifice. Eventually, there will be less fear and more and faster progress toward other things you try. Success is a reward, a return on sacrifice.

CONCLUSION

21

The Next Level: Shoot for the Moon!

'We are what we repeatedly do.
Excellence, then, is not an act, but a habit'
~ Aristotle

Now that you've worked through the first two parts of this book, let's look both backwards at what you did, as well as forward to what more you can accomplish.

If you have worked through five or six of the chapters in Part II, the "Taking Action" section, you should be well on your way to success—at least seeing some significant change. But now you are at a crossroads. Do you want to get off the train at this stop, or do you want to excel further and strive for another goal?

When I say, do you want to get off the train, I'm acknowledging that many people set a goal and are ready to stop when they arrive at that goal. In this chapter, I'm talking to those who want to reach higher and see where the next adventure goes. If you want to go further, you will need to assess where you have been and where you are, as well as make a new set of plans and goals. Are you ready, willing and looking for another chapter in your life?

First step: Go back and reread the chapter on peers, friends and family and reassess where you are today regarding these relationships. List the five people closest to you. Are you still listing the same five people from years ago, or have you added a couple of new people and find yourself spending less time with one or two people in your previous list? Have you taken a similar path placing yourself in either completely or partly in a new environment to move yourself out of your comfort zone?

Next, reset your dreams and desires. Where do you want to go?

When you did personal assessments in Part I, one of the tasks was to review your weaknesses and reduce those to the degree that they would no longer impede your progress. Well, now you are in a new place and you will usually find that it's time to reassess things. Some skill that might have been "OK" in getting to where you are now might no longer be sufficient for your next stage or your next goal. Based on your next goal, there may be an improvement needed in some skill that was sufficient for your current success. Furthermore, there may a new skill you need that requires at least acceptable proficiency. For example, you may be outgoing, but are you ready to speak in public or make presentations? Are you comfortable in front of a camera, if interviewed? Are you in a position now that necessitates going out to dinner at high-end restaurants? To make further progress, you may have to confront a weakness today that was not there previously.

Go back and review the chapter on copying well. While this certainly should be the easiest of any of the requisite skills for success, in my experience people rarely do it well, and they usually can't even repeat back exactly what the successful person did or said. So go back for two reasons. First, assess as how well you followed the advice in the last step of your progress. Second, find a mentor whose success or status you would like to duplicate. Take a look at whom or what you may follow in your next stage toward success.

It's also time to reflect on the successes you've already achieved. This is not just for now, but for every time in the future that you go through this process. Over time, repeated successes will eventually lead to a "I can do anything, just show me the path," attitude. So don't forget to celebrate or congratulate yourself. After repeated successes, what you have started to gain is a skill in mastering the Mechanics for Breakthrough Success.

You should take comfort in seeing how far you've come, but don't live in the past. Spend most of your time looking forward to the next challenge, the next goal, and the next success. When you do this, you are combining a resounding pride in your successes with confidence and belief in your next journey.

What is the difference between being extremely successful and just good? I believe most of it is hard work, dedication and perseverance. For much of this process, you need to build repeated successes along with being ready to move forward whenever you near a goal. Remember the story from my introduction. If somebody has a 100 IQ and you had a 90, given that we supposedly use 10% of our brain, if you work 20% harder than they do, you will be at a 10.8 mental performance level while they will be at a 10 mental performance level. Also, with repeated successes over time, you could feel that in many fields there really wasn't anything you couldn't achieve if you wanted it.

Identify the *top* people in your profession or business. Re-aim your sites to be Number 1. Why? If you aim to be in the top 10, you'll be lucky to make five or six. But if you aim for Number 1 you're very likely to know how to make it to at least the top 2 or 3.

That said, keep in mind that success is not absolute, it is relative. Think about how you make changes over time. Any progress you make is expanding your opportunities and skill levels. This includes the notion of wealth; it, too, is a relative concept. Most people who become rich get there slowly and through discipline. It is not where you are that is important, but rather where you came from and where you're going that brings happiness and satisfaction.

Furthermore, you should not be comparing yourself to others unless it's to learn from them. If you find any jealousy rearing its ugly head, remember that jealousy is just a signal to learn from the other person what you can. Soak up information and constantly shop for knowledge. Listen, listen, listen! As I've said before, you can learn from everyone, not just your mentors. Observe everything around you. Watch how dogs can be more persistent than humans in order to get their way. And recall my earlier story about how babies learn to walk. It takes them many months of falling down banging their head and face in order to finally succeed. Can you have more persistence and dedication than a baby? Is there anything you should quit trying to do, when it takes only a few months and will have a massive effect on your future?

Your success belongs to you, and you alone. Your personal preference as to how far or where you go is made up of your own actions, wants and needs. That means that your eventual happiness is decided by your choices. Thus, the only comparison you should make is with yourself, as you're the only person who truly understands what you know and what you don't know. You can be your own best critic. Look at yourself and analyze within your specialty, what don't you know? Let me say that again, slightly differently. Most people worry about what they need to know to accomplish whatever goal they have, rather than what they *don't know*. If you concentrate on what you don't know, you will far outperform any expectations.

At the same time, you do become a product of where you hang out. Your success, while ultimately yours alone, is influenced by the opinions of others and where they think you can go. People see you through their own perceptual filters and from the perspective of their own comfort zone. Your fate, income, wealth, living style and environment are often largely determined by those five peers, friends and family mentioned earlier. Even given the "Five Friends Rule," it is still your decision whether to keep these friends or move on to new friends. You can continue to grow until you decide to stop, but that decision is yours and should never be the decision of your "friends."

Part of moving ahead on your journey to repeated successes—however you define them—is the *thought process* of becoming extremely successful. One thing you may have to do, is change your own perception of yourself. Just like you break habits such as smoking, overeating or yes, overindulging in TV, you may need to make some fundamental changes. Those changes include your outlook towards your own future, as well as the aforementioned environment, friends and peers you keep. While continuing to seek new higher goals may seem difficult, it will get easier and easier over time as your successes multiply. It will also become more fun. It truly becomes your own game as you reach higher, achieve success and celebrate.

Now let me caution about a hole you could fall into while striving for higher goals. This hole is what I refer to as "making decisions too early"—that is, before it's necessary to do so. Here's an example of what I mean:

Most people develop opinions—deciding whether something is good, better or useful—based on what they observe at the time. There can be a major problem with this. Faced with a problem, you have to make a decision--usually yes or no, go or no-go. Imagine that the data regarding this problem show up as 34 items in favor of making a certain decision and 22 against doing so. It could be the best approaches to eat healthy eating, like choosing margarine or butter, skimmed milk or whole milk, or avoiding coffee and whole eggs. Or it could be about the best way to do something, like learning a language. Most people seeing this will decide in favor of the 34 pieces of data. But you should keep an open mind. Don't cast final judgment unless it is absolutely necessary. You might follow a suggestion, but don't immediately close the door on new information.

Let's say, for example, that you don't have to make a decision until sometime next year. During that period, you could be receiving one piece of information at a time. If you had already decided in favor of a particular decision, each piece of new information will be weighed not against all the collective data, but rather against your previous decision—and that decision will almost always be successfully defended against one piece of additional data. But if you had waited until the decision was necessary and all that data was in, you might actually see a new collective tally of 39 pieces of data in favor of a decision and 52 against. I've seen this scenario many times. Think about it: How many times have you had difficulty convincing somebody else of something that you knew was true and could logically explain it, but they just wouldn't listen or just couldn't understand you? Why couldn't they understand? Did *they* make their decision too early and were unable to listen to new information? Don't make that mistake yourself.

As you move forward through various levels of success you may need to go back several times to review various chapters. These principles are universal at any level, and you will find them useful because you are bound to change your mindset and goals many times over the course of your life. That's okay! New ideas, new opportunities and outside influences may well change the feasibility or the desire for your current goal. You will need to reassess. But don't worry. The process of learning and growing, as well as the specific skills acquired as part of that process, will open up many more opportunities, and you will find them useful regardless of how your path changes over time. In a sense, you are now in the process of rebranding yourself in your own mind.

This material will continue to be updated and I would love to know how you are doing. Some of these suggestions are quite difficult to implement and may need more of an explanation. So now, go to the web site and get the information that was not available at this printing and send me a note of any comments you have or wishes for future additions or explanations.

And thank you for daring to take this journey to "Breakthrough Success"!

****

Stay in touch and contact me through:
The website: http://MechanicsForSuccess.com
The Podcast: Life Unsettled on iTunes, Stitcher (Android) and Google Play Music
The Podcast website: http://LifeUnsettled.com
Sign up for updates or new handouts!

~ *Thomas O'Grady, PhD*

www.ingramcontent.com/pod-product-compliance
Lightning Source LLC
Chambersburg PA
CBHW061633040426
42446CB00010B/1396